DONALD TRUMP

From Real Estate to Reality TV

Sara McIntosh Wooten

Enslow Publishers, Inc.
40 Industrial Road
Box 398
Berkeley Heights, NJ 07922
USA

http://www.enslow.com

Library of Congress Cataloging-in-Publication Data

Wooten, Sara McIntosh.
    Donald Trump : from real estate to reality TV / Sara McIntosh Wooten.
        p. cm. — (People to know today)
    Summary: "A biography of real estate tycoon Donald Trump"—Provided by publisher.
    Includes bibliographical references and index.
    ISBN-13: 978-0-7660-2890-6
    ISBN-10: 0-7660-2890-9
    1. Trump, Donald, 1946—-Juvenile literature. 2. Businesspeople—United States—
Biography—Juvenile literature. 3. Real estate developers—United States—Biography—Juvenile
literature. I. Title.
    HC102.5.T78W66 2008
    333.33092—dc22
    [B]   2007018106

Printed in the United States of America

10 9 8 7 6 5 4 3 2 1

To Our Readers: We have done our best to make sure all Internet addresses in this book were
active and appropriate when we went to press. However, the author and publisher have no control
over and assume no liability for the material available on those Internet sites or on other Web sites
they may link to. Any comments or suggestions can be sent by e-mail to comments@enslow.com
or to the address on the back cover.

♻ Enslow Publishers, Inc., is committed to printing our books on recycled paper. The paper in
every book contains 10% to 30% post-consumer waste (PCW). The cover board on the outside of
each book contains 100% PCW. Our goal is to do our part to help young people and the
environment too!

Cover Illustration: AP/Wide World Photos, pp. 1, 4, 9, 38, 67, 75, 84, 99, 101, 104;
Thomas Barrat/Shutterstock, p. 96; Tommy Baynard/© NBC/Courtesy Everett
Collection, p. 95; Trevor Boyd/iStockphoto, p. 53; Richard Corkery/New York Daily
News, p. 59; © NBC/Courtesy Everett Collection, p. 6; New York Daily News, p. 36;
New York Military Academy Archives, p. 18; Newscom, p. 80; Barton Silverman/The
New York Times/Redux, p. 28; Time & Life Pictures/Getty Images, p. 15; Courtesy of
The Trump Organization, p. 13; WireImage/Getty Images, pp. 40, 51.

Photos and Illustrations: AP/Wide World Photos.

CONTENTS

Donald Trump

"You're Fired!"

In late August 2003, sixteen strangers from across the country gathered in New York City. From the first, things moved quickly. Within one hour they had met one another, checked out the luxury apartment they would be living in together for the next few months, and were given their first business assignment.[1]

All in their twenties or thirties, the eight women and eight men were very different from one another. For example, some were instant leaders and jumped in from the start to give the rest of the group directions. Others, on the other hand, were more comfortable taking a low-key role. Some were natural team players; others worked better by themselves. Some had college and advanced education degrees; others had begun their careers right after high school. And all of them had different career and business experiences, including real estate, sales, and consulting. Yet, besides the fact that all sixteen were at least reasonably successful in their careers, this group of strangers had one other thing in common. They had become the first set of participants in the first season of a new reality show, *The Apprentice*.

Why would these sixteen people, chosen from approximately 215,000 applicants, be willing to take themselves out of their normal lives, away from their homes, families, and businesses for several months? Why would they agree to put themselves on a television show where they would be stressed, humiliated, and tested in front of millions of viewers? They were willing because the final winner would walk away with the

Donald Trump stands front and center, flanked by the sixteen contestants of the first season of *The Apprentice*, which aired in 2004.

opportunity to run one of Donald Trump's companies for a year—with a salary of $250,000!

From the first, the participants were divided into two teams—men against women. The men called their team Versacorp; the women became the Protégé Corporation. In the weeks ahead, the teams would receive a new business assignment every two or three days. It might be selling lemonade to downtown New Yorkers or developing an advertising campaign for a hot new product. Another time, each team had to manage a restaurant for an evening. Over the entire first season, the teams would complete thirteen different business assignments.

At the end of every task, each team's profits were counted. After all, making money is what business is all about. Whichever team had made the most money won. They were rewarded with a special treat, such as a fancy dinner at an exclusive New York City

High Standards

Focusing on high-dollar Manhattan real estate at the beginning, Donald Trump's empire of moneymaking business deals has grown from hotels and apartment buildings to golf courses and casino-hotels across the country. As chairman and president of the Trump Organization, most of his holdings bear his name. And he demands that with his name on them, all his properties must maintain the highest possible standards of luxury and quality.[2]

restaurant or the chance to meet a famous celebrity or sports star.

The losing team, on the other hand, had to pack their bags and face Donald Trump in his eerily dark, richly furnished boardroom. After a long session of grueling questions, finger-pointing, backstabbing, and excuses about why their team had lost, one contestant would see Trump's forefinger point at him or her and hear the dreaded words, "You're fired!" At that point, the loser was left to slink off to a waiting cab, suitcase in hand, to be whisked to the airport and back home.

So, who is Donald Trump? How is he able to command so much respect that he can have his own reality show with hundreds of thousands of applicants clamoring for a chance to work for him?

> "I've got a **big ego. Every successful person has.**"

Since buying his first Manhattan (downtown New York City) property in 1974 at the age of twenty-eight, Donald Trump has become one of the world's most well-known and successful entrepreneurs. An entrepreneur is a person who starts his or her own business.

In addition to his business dealings, Trump has also written a number of books, many of which have become best sellers. And Trump has now expanded his ventures by becoming a well-known and highly successful television personality with his hit show, *The Apprentice*.

A controversial figure, Donald Trump is definitely not without his critics. While many admire him as one of the world's most talented and successful businessmen, others find him obnoxious and egotistical.[3] As Trump himself has written: "I've got a big ego. Every successful person has."[4]

Regardless, he is a master at getting publicity and aggressively promoting his business projects. And like

Bill Rancic (right) won the first season of *The Apprentice*. He and Trump are pictured attending the demolition ceremonies of the old Chicago *Sun-Times* building. The new Trump International Hotel and Tower will take its place along the Chicago River.

him or not, Donald Trump remains a force to reckon with in the world of high-stakes real estate.

The first season of *The Apprentice* was a big success. It became the hottest new television show of that season.[5] Each week, television viewers rooted for their favorite candidates and bit their fingernails as they watched the pressure the contestants battled as the eliminations continued. The show's success surprised even its most enthusiastic supporters, with the episodes averaging more than twenty million viewers.[6]

By the end of the season, fourteen hopefuls had been sent packing, and only two remained. Finally, with the last task completed and in front of forty million live viewers, one contestant heard the happy words, "You're hired!" Bill Rancic, himself an entrepreneur from Chicago, Illinois, was chosen by Trump to oversee the construction of his latest building project in Chicago, a giant skyscraper to be named the Trump International Hotel and Tower.

Since that first season, *The Apprentice* continued to enjoy large television audiences as it moved into its sixth season in January 2007. At the same time, Donald Trump continues to build his empire and his reputation as one of America's most famous (and controversial) entrepreneurs.

2
A BORN COMPETITOR

Donald John Trump was born on June 14, 1946, in Queens, New York. Queens is a mainly middle-class borough, or section, southeast of downtown New York City. He was the fourth child in a family which would ultimately include five children. The oldest was a daughter named Maryanne, who was followed by Fred, Jr., called Freddy, and then Elizabeth. Next came Donald, and two years later, his younger brother, Robert.

Donald grew up with the highest regard and admiration for his parents, later proclaiming, "I got very lucky in having Fred and Mary as parents. I could not have done any better."[1]

Fred's life had been a tough one, especially with his father's death from pneumonia when Fred was just thirteen years old. While his mother earned money as a seamstress, Fred, as the oldest son, was needed to help support his family financially. He was hardworking and enterprising, and soon took on odd jobs, including working on construction sites where he helped build houses. Finding that he enjoyed building, Fred also took evening classes in construction while he was still in high school.

By the time he was eighteen, Fred and his mother had formed a company called Elizabeth Trump & Son, to develop and manage real estate. Fred needed his mother's help because at eighteen, he was too young to sign business contracts. He built his first home one year after graduating from high school, and he used the money he made when he sold it to build another home. Before long, Fred was in the business of building and selling homes in Queens. He specialized in building small brick homes that were reasonably priced. And his business only continued to expand. He either built new homes or bought and renovated, or updated, homes that had been abandoned, turning them into rental properties. He made sure they were maintained well and enjoyed the

A Typical Family

The Trump family was typical for that time—a two-parent household in which his mother, Mary, stayed home and cared for the house and the children, while her husband, Fred, worked an outside job as a real estate developer. As Donald later wrote: "My father was the power and the breadwinner, and my mother was the perfect housewife."[2]

Donald Trump as a toddler
in the late 1940s.

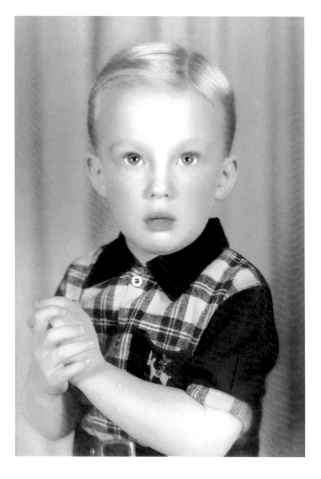

monthly rental money
that kept growing in his
bank account.

By the time Donald
was born, Fred had
become a very successful
real-estate developer. In
addition to single-family
homes, he also began to
build, or buy and reno-
vate, large middle-class
apartment complexes in
Queens and the Bronx,
another nearby borough
of New York City.

With a growing family, Fred also built a large
two-story home for them on Midland Parkway in
Queens. An imposing two-story brick home with a
large porch supported by four tall white columns, the
house had twenty-three rooms and nine bathrooms.
Fred now had plenty of room for his growing children.
As his business and wealth continued to grow over
the years, the family also enjoyed the services of a
maid, along with a chauffeur who drove their Cadillac
limousine.

But success had its price for Fred. Donald remembers his father working constantly, from before dawn until after dark each day, seldom ever taking a day off. Not content to just sit back and pocket his monthly rental money, Fred knew that being successful meant keeping his properties well taken care of. And for him, that meant frequent personal inspections.

As Donald grew older, he would often go with his father on weekends and school vacations to check on his properties. Together they would collect rents, inspect work in progress, and make sure everything was in excellent condition. Donald also had the job of scouting the ground for unused nails that could be recycled rather than wasted.

All the while, Donald watched his father's behavior as a businessman, and it started to take hold. He began to learn how to run a business well—that it took constant attention and a lot of hard work.[3]

Donald also learned the value of a dollar by watching his father stretch his resources. For example, Fred might spray his apartment buildings for insects himself rather than paying someone to do it for him. Donald also saw his father's reputation grow as a solid, dependable real estate developer.[4]

Even though the Trump children grew up in relative wealth and in a large home, they did not feel particularly "rich."[5] Fred and Mary were determined not to spoil their children. They all had chores to do,

Fred Trump may have been serious when it came to his business, but he also knew how to have fun. Here he is having a good time at a square dance he had for the tenants of one of his housing projects in 1951.

and when they were old enough, all were required to get part-time jobs. Their parents ran a tight, structured household with lots of rules. Money was not wasted on extra toys or frills.[6]

Top behavior was also expected from the Trump children.[7] Mary would report to Fred each evening about their children's behavior that day, and bad reports led to swift punishment. Neither were the Trump children allowed to own any pets. They had to go to their next door neighbor's, the MacIntosh's, to get treats such as cookies or to cuddle their neighbor's cats and rabbits. The Trumps also taught their children to think positively, even when times were bad, and never to quit a job they had begun.[8]

As a boy growing up in the Trump household, Donald was full of energy and ambition. His older brother, Freddy, was not born with quite the same drive or killer instincts that Donald had. Instead, Freddy had a good sense of humor, enjoyed many friendships, and wanted to be liked. Their father saw Freddy as "soft" and did not respect him.[9] He would constantly find fault with his oldest son's behavior and abilities, trying to make him tougher. Donald observed those harsh lessons and quickly learned what his father expected.[10] With his energy and ability to stand up to his father, Donald earned his father's respect. They would maintain a very close relationship for the rest of Fred's life.[11]

Among his siblings, Donald was closest to his younger brother, Robert. Together they would play with blocks, each building his own skyscrapers and houses. Once, while playing with their blocks, Donald needed to borrow some of Robert's blocks to build an extra tall skyscraper. But rather than returning the borrowed blocks to his brother when he was through, Donald glued the pieces of his skyscraper together so he would never have to give them back.[12] The incident served to predict Donald's ability to get what he wanted, a trait which would remain with him throughout his life.

Over time, Donald grew into a tall, blond young boy. Along with his siblings, he attended Kew Forest, a private school about twenty minutes from the Trump home. He was not an excellent student, finishing in the bottom half of his elementary-school class. But he made up for low academics by excelling in athletics. Regardless of the sport, Donald proved to be a very competitive player, driven to win.[13]

He was also somewhat of a discipline problem at Kew Forest. For example, he might set off a stink bomb in class, send spitballs flying across a classroom, or disrespectfully talk back to a teacher. Once, he was almost expelled for punching his music teacher in the face.[14] As his older sister Maryanne remembered of that time, "He [Donald] was a brat."[15]

Getting bad reports about their son's behavior at school did not please his parents. So when Donald was thirteen, they enrolled him in the New York Military Academy, a college preparatory boarding school about fifty-five miles north of New York City. Donald did not like the idea of attending military school.[16] But his father believed the academy would channel his son's energy in a more productive way. He hoped that in a military environment Donald would develop the self-discipline he needed.[17]

Life was tightly structured at the academy. The students, or cadets as they were called, had to wear military uniforms every day. They got up each morning before dawn to the piercing sound of a bugle, marched to their classes, and were expected to attend regular chapel services. While there, Donald was nicknamed "D.T." by his classmates.

Donald easily could have rebelled against his new-found structure and limits. But luckily, he responded well. His father had been right. The new challenges at the academy tapped into Donald's competitive nature, and he drove himself to become

the best cadet there.[18] The athletic opportunities the academy offered appealed to Donald as well. While there he played football, soccer, basketball, and baseball. He earned a reputation as an outstanding first baseman, and led the baseball team as its captain his senior year.[19] Meanwhile, Fred and Mary visited their son on

Donald Trump's senior portrait from the New York Military Academy, 1964.

weekends, watching as he matured. His high energy and training develop into self-confidence and leadership ability.[20]

After graduating from New York Military Academy in 1964, Donald spent his next two years at Fordham University, a small men's school in the Bronx. At Fordham, he majored in business administration. While attending classes at Fordham, he lived at home and made reasonably good grades. He also put his athletic skills to use once again, playing squash, football, and tennis.

After two years at Fordham, Donald transferred to the University of Pennsylvania's Wharton School. Nationally known as one of the top business schools in the country, Wharton was yet another structured environment for Donald. Besides tough classes, Wharton had a formal atmosphere; its students had to wear coats and ties to classes. While there, Donald concentrated on real-estate classes. By the time he graduated from Wharton in 1968 with a bachelor's degree in economics, Donald was ready to begin his career.

3
AN ABLE APPRENTICE

Fred had always hoped that at least one of his sons would join him in his real estate business.[1] Even so, he had encouraged his children to choose their careers based on what they were passionate about.[2] And although Donald had briefly considered a career as a baseball player or as an actor earlier in his life, by the time he graduated from Wharton, he knew his destiny lay in real estate.[3]

During this time, the United States was at war with North Vietnam in Southeast Asia. All men between the ages of eighteen and thirty-five faced the possibility of being drafted, or called upon by the government, to serve in the armed forces to help with the war effort. Once he graduated from Wharton, Trump became eligible for the draft. But in September 1968, he was excused from any military obligation. Based on his physical examination by the draft office, he received a medical deferment. That meant that for medical reasons, he was excused from military duty.[4]

For the next five years, Donald Trump worked directly with his father, learning more and more about the real-estate business. He lived at home for the first three years. Together, every morning he and his father would go out to the Trump office on Avenue Z in the Bronx in Fred's chauffeur-driven limousine.

Always frugal and non-showy, Fred's office suited him just fine. Despite his wealth, he maintained a very low-key, nondescript place of business in a three-story-brick building. Divided into cubicles, which served as offices for his employees, the Trump headquarters sported outdated 1950s furniture, a few plastic plants for decoration, linoleum floors, and shag carpeting.

Donald's addition to the company was just what his father had always hoped for.[5] His older son, Freddy, had tried to work for his father, but that had not gone well. Tough himself, Fred expected his sons to be, too—especially in business.[6] Still ever critical of his oldest son, Fred continually criticized Freddy for not being tough enough to be a successful businessman.[7]

Over time, the pressure and misery of working for his father became unbearable for Freddy. For comfort, he turned to smoking cigarettes and drinking alcohol excessively, which only made his father more furious.[8]

Once again, just as when he was a boy, Donald watched and learned from Freddy's mistakes. Observing his older brother's addictions to cigarettes and alcohol, he resolved never to drink alcohol or smoke himself, resolutions which he has kept throughout his life.

Eventually, Freddy left the real-estate business and moved to Florida, where he became an airline pilot. He left the job of working for Fred to his younger brother Donald, who was ready to go to work. As a friend of his father's noticed early on, Donald Trump's eagerness to get to work and make a name for himself was obvious. And in contrast to his father, who was always all business and serious, Donald Trump had a more open and friendly air about him.[9]

Working at his father's side over the next five years, Donald Trump's duties mainly involved collecting rents and making sure the Trump properties were in top condition. Fred also used that time to complete his son's education in the art of successful real-estate development.[10] There was a lot to learn, but Donald Trump was a quick study.

Among his lessons, Fred taught his son how to collect rent from reluctant or even dangerous tenants. He learned the ins and outs of maintenance contracts and how to get the best deals on supplies. Fred also showed his son how to make all kinds of building repairs, so he would not have to hire a highly paid worker to do them.

In addition, Fred also taught his son how to negotiate successfully with workers and unions, and how to be tough to get his projects completed on time and within budget. Over time, Donald Trump learned all the complexities of New York City real estate development, such as how to borrow money from banks to build a project, and how to deal successfully with the city zoning commissioners, whose job was

> **"I learned about motivating people, and I learned about competence and efficiency."**

to approve or deny new building proposals. He learned how to promote his projects and how to handle public opposition if that happened. And he learned the importance of using business contacts and political connections to his advantage.[11] As Donald Trump would later sum it up, "I learned about toughness [from my father] in a very tough business, I learned about motivating people, and I learned about competence and efficiency."[12]

Fred was also very careful about his appearance, another trait that his son would take on. Every day the two men wore suits or coats and ties, even on weekends. Fred made sure his son knew that a professional image was critical to a successful business.[13]

In 1971, Donald Trump took the first step toward moving his career and dreams forward. He moved out of his family home on Midland Parkway and into a studio apartment in the Upper East Side of Manhattan. Living on the seventeenth floor of a twenty-one-story building, he called his tiny, dark new home with no view of the city his "penthouse."[14]

Despite his modest dwelling, he was absolutely thrilled. "Moving into that apartment," he would later write, "was probably more exciting for me than moving, fifteen years later, into the top three floors of Trump Tower."[15] On his own for the first time, Donald Trump finally felt like he had entered the adult world, and he was proud to live in New York City.[16] He also knew that he was where he needed to be to fulfill the next part of his dream—to get into big-time Manhattan real estate, selling to the world's wealthiest people.[17]

Trump drove in style as well, owning a white Cadillac convertible. On the back bumper his customized license plate was printed with his initials—DJT. Each day, he would drive from Manhattan out to the Trump Organization office on Avenue Z in the Bronx and return to Manhattan against rush-hour traffic each evening.

He also joined a posh private club in Manhattan called Le Club on East Fifty-eighth Street. Membership at Le Club meant success for him. He knew it would become a great place to meet and network with other businessmen, lawyers, bankers, and real estate-developers—people who could help with his career.[18]

In 1972, Fred gave Donald the job of selling one of his apartment complexes in Cincinnati, Ohio. He had bought the complex in 1964, when his son was attending Fordham University. Built in the 1950s, the complex consisted of twelve hundred units, and it was one of the largest apartment complexes Cincinnati had to offer. It was called Swifton Village.

When Fred bought Swifton Village, most other real-estate developers in the area thought it was a bad deal. The complex had not been well taken care of and had become rundown over the years. Many of the apartment units were vacant. But where others saw a disaster, Fred saw a great business opportunity.

He set to work hiring contractors to fix up the complex. Donald became familiar with the project and sometimes would fly over to Cincinnati with his father on weekends to help supervise and inspect the improvements as they progressed. Before long, with the help of fresh paint, new appliances, white shutters at the windows, and updated landscaping, new renters began flocking to the apartment complex.

But by the fall of 1972, Fred was ready to sell Swifton Village. The surrounding neighborhoods had declined, and many of his renters had decided to move elsewhere. By this time, he had enough confidence in his son's abilities to put him in charge of getting the complex sold. Before long, a possible buyer, Prudent Real Estate Investment Trust, contacted Donald Trump to discuss the property. With the help of another apartment manager from the area, Trump convinced the Prudent representative that Swifton Village would be a great property to buy.[19] At twenty-six years of age, Donald Trump had successfully completed his first multimillion-dollar sale. It would be the first of many.

Over time, he would occasionally offer his father business suggestions. Some his father took advantage of; others he did not. For example, Donald Trump convinced his father to refinance, or get new loans, for a number of his properties. That resulted in a savings of tens of thousands of dollars for the Trump Organization.

But there was one piece of advice Donald was set on, while his father refused to budge: moving into Manhattan real estate. Fred was comfortable working the areas he was familiar with—Queens and the Bronx—where property values were reasonable, and most people had middle-class values and tastes.[20] But his son's sights were set on the glitz and glamour of Manhattan, home of some of the most expensive real estate in the world. "It [Manhattan real estate] wasn't his thing," Donald later said about his father in an interview.[21] Yet Donald Trump remained drawn by the allure of Manhattan. "I learned very early on that I didn't want to be in the business my father was in [Queens and Brooklyn real estate]. I wanted to try something grander, more glamorous, and more exciting."[22]

In 1973, the U.S. Justice Department filed a lawsuit against the Trump Organization for discriminating against African Americans. The suit alleged that the Trump properties would not rent to African Americans, either falsely claiming that no apartments were available or quoting high rental rates, which they knew the African-Americans applicants could not afford. Fred had faced charges such as those years before but had settled out of court with minimal publicity.[23] This time, however, his son took over and chose to confront the issue directly and publicly.

True to the style for which he would become famous, Donald Trump called a press conference. He denied the charges and announced a countersuit against the government for one hundred milliondollars in damages against the Trump Organization. The case was finally settled two years later. By that time, Donald Trump's charges against the government had long been thrown out. The final ruling required the Trumps to advertise their apartments in a newspaper with a high African-Americans readership; update the Urban League, a civil rights organization; on apartment vacancies, and count welfare payments when they were checking a possible tenant's income.

By 1973, Fred was so pleased with his son's abilities as his assistant that he named him president of the company. Fred kept the title of chairman of the board. Up to this time, Fred had called his company a variety of names, such as the Trump Village Construction Corporation or, in Cincinnati, The Swifton Land Corporation.[24] Donald Trump convinced his father to formalize and finalize the name of the family company as

Donald Trump stands with his father, Fred, at Trump Village in Brooklyn, 1973. At twenty-seven years old, Donald Trump became president of the Trump Organization.

the Trump Organization. It was simple and clear and remains the name of the company to this day.

Since his move to Manhattan, Donald Trump had kept constant watch on available real estate, waiting to find the right property for the right price. It had taken two years, but in 1973, the chance he had been waiting for opened up. Trump's career in high-end real estate was on the brink of taking off.

4

THE BIG TIME

In 1973, New York City, as well as the entire state of New York, was in a financial decline. In fact, the city was on the verge of bankruptcy. That meant they were close to not having enough money to pay their employees or their bills. Manhattan real estate was in a slump as well. Yet, Trump was not discouraged. He later wrote of that time: "I saw the city's trouble as a great opportunity for me."[1]

And he was right. One day, while looking over *The New York Times* newspaper, Trump saw an article that caught his eye. The Penn Central Railroad had declared bankruptcy and was looking to sell its many properties, a number of which were in New York City.[2] Trump knew that with the company in financial distress, they would probably be willing to sell their holdings at a good price.

So he called Penn Central's agent, Victor Palmieri, to find out more about the railroad's available property in New York City. One was an empty rail yard at Thirty-fourth Street; another was a rail yard at Sixtieth Street.

Over time, Trump convinced Palmieri to grant him the option to buy both rail yards. That meant that when it came time to actually develop, or build on, the properties, Trump would be the first to get the chance to buy them.

In working those deals, Trump was lucky. A complete unknown in the world of New York City real estate, he was a risky candidate to sell to. But he had several things going for him. First, his father's reputation as a dependable real-estate developer added to his credibility. Second, his energy and determination made a big positive impression on Palmieri. And finally, no other more qualified candidates came forward to make offers on the properties.[3]

Trump had big plans for his new acquisitions. Between the two rail yards, he wanted to build a total of thirty thousand middle-income apartments in high-rise buildings. But he met with immediate opposition from the city planners who had to approve his proposal. Practically everyone thought Trump's idea was over-the-top and ridiculous.[4]

After fighting long and hard for city approval over the next several years, Trump finally released his option on the Thirty-fourth Street yards back to Penn Central. They then sold the property to the city, which used it to build a new convention center. It would be years before Trump's plans for the Sixtieth Street rail yard could go forward.

In the meantime, Trump's attention was caught by yet another Penn Central property, the Commodore Hotel on Forty-second Street. The Commodore had a long and glorious history. In its prime it had been regarded as one of New York City's finest landmarks.[5] The sixty-five-year-old hotel had been named for railroad businessman Cornelius (also known as Commodore) Vanderbilt. With 2,500 rooms, it was one of the largest hotels in New York City.

But since its heyday, the Commodore had fallen on hard times. Without enough money from Penn Central to keep it in good shape, the once grand hotel had become an eyesore. In fact, the whole area around Grand Central Terminal had fallen into decline. By the time the hotel got Trump's attention, it was run-down and dirty and surrounded by empty buildings and boarded-up storefronts. Few of its rooms were rented, and rumor

The Commodore

The Commodore was located across from Grand Central Terminal (often called Grand Central Station), the largest railroad station in the world. Because of that, the Commodore was in an excellent place to take advantage of the thousands of potential customers who flocked to the city each day on the trains that whizzed in and out of the station.

had it that a section of the hotel was used to house a prostitution ring.[6] Despite the Commodore's problems, Donald Trump saw it as a huge opportunity. He wanted to transform it back into the city's most glamorous hotel.[7]

But where Trump saw opportunity, practically everyone else saw disaster. His father, Fred, along with many others, told him they thought he was crazy to even consider buying the pitiful property.[8]

Yet Trump was not discouraged. He knew there were many obstacles in his path, including getting city approvals. But he was not about to give up. As he would later write: "Winners see problems as just another way to prove themselves."[9] Instead, he focused on the possibility of success. If he were able to transform the Commodore and make it profitable, it would jump-start his reputation as a successful Manhattan real-estate developer. He also knew that if the hotel did well, it would provide thousands of construction and service jobs for the city, and it would go a long way toward reversing the downturn of the entire Forty-second Street area.[10]

> **"Winners** see problems as just another way to **prove** themselves."

Trump hired a lawyer, George Ross, to help him through the complexities he would need to overcome to make his plans for the hotel a reality. He also hired a well-known and respected architect, named Der

Scutt, to develop a design for the hotel's new look. Trump next needed to find a good hotel chain to partner with him in the Commodore project. Since he had no experience in hotel management, his job would be to renovate the hotel; theirs would be to manage it.

Trump contacted the Hyatt Hotel organization to see if they might be interested. He knew that the Hyatt chain was known for its quality, service, spectacular architecture, and profitable convention business.[11] In addition, they did not already have a hotel in New York City.

In their talks with Trump, representatives from the Hyatt were not delighted with the New York City location he was proposing. Yet they knew he was also working on getting the Commodore a big tax break from the city, which would save them a lot of money. So they agreed that if the project did, indeed, go forward, they would partner with Trump.

The tax-break issue was critical. It would make or break the entire Commodore deal. To get it, Trump needed a big favor from the city of New York. He asked for a tax abatement for the hotel for the next forty years. That would mean that the hotel's owners would not have to pay property taxes on it during that time. If granted, it would save the hotel tens of millions of dollars. In exchange for the tax break, Trump offered the city a share in the hotel's profits. The city officials were very reluctant to grant Trump a tax abatement.

With the city nearly broke, they desperately needed the tax dollars a profitable hotel would provide. Also, once other hotel owners got wind of Trump's proposal, they protested, saying it would not be fair for the Commodore to get a tax break when they did not.[12]

Along with the tax issue, Trump also needed to find a bank that would loan him the money to renovate the hotel. In all, he needed seventy million dollars. But again, due to the city's strapped finances, banks were reluctant to loan money for any building project, much less to an unknown and untested real-estate developer. Bank after bank turned him down. If they lent him the money and the Commodore project failed, they could lose all the money they had loaned him. So Trump continued to hammer away at the tax abatement issue. If he were successful with that, he thought a bank might be more willing to lend him money.[13]

The turning point with the city came in May 1976 when Penn Central announced its plan to completely close the Commodore in just six days.[14] That prompted the city to act in Trump's favor. The last thing they wanted was the negative publicity of a well-known hotel shutting down in the city. In addition, Trump and his father had strong connections with the governor of New York at the time, Hugh Carey, along with the mayor of New York City, Abe Beame.[15] With their backing, the tax abatement was approved. That

Trump shows a sketch of the Commodore renovation to New York City Economic Development Administrator Alfred Eisenpreis in 1976.

breakthrough paved the way for the bank loans Donald Trump needed.

In the meantime, since his move to Manhattan in 1971, Trump had not taken the time to include romance in his life. He sometimes dated models he met at Le Club, but none had turned into a serious relationship. He was too focused on getting his career off the ground.[16] But his social life changed dramatically in the summer of 1976. Still not a serious dater, one night Trump stopped in at Maxwell's Plum, a popular restaurant on the Upper East Side, for dinner. As fate would have it, that night he happened to cross paths with a strikingly beautiful, twenty-seven-year-old blonde model from

Canada, named Ivana Marie Zelnickova Winklmayr. She, along with several other models, were trying to get a table at the crowded restaurant. Trump came to their rescue, not only getting them a table, but also picking up their bill. After later escorting the ladies back to their hotel, Trump sent Ivana a dozen roses the next day. He was smitten.[17]

Ivana had immigrated to Canada from Czechoslovakia (now the Czech Republic) three years earlier, where she became a successful fashion model. When she met Trump, she was in New York City for a modeling assignment. Shortly after they met, the couple began to date whenever she was in the city. And Trump did everything he could to sweep her off her feet.[18]

As he got to know her better, Trump found that he and Ivana shared many of the same qualities. Like him, she was self-confident, competitive, and driven to excel.[19] She also had a tremendous amount of energy, and was quite intelligent.[20] That fall, he took her to Queens to meet his parents.

An expert skier, Ivana was involved with another man, named George Syrovatka, when she met Trump. Like her, he was also an excellent skier who sold sports equipment in Montreal, Canada. He had been responsible for helping Ivana emigrate from Czechoslovakia. But Trump, used to getting what he wanted, turned Ivana's head. At twenty-seven, she was ready to get married, and she knew George was not.[21] So when Trump proposed on New Year's Eve, 1976, Ivana said yes.

The couple was married on April 9, 1977, at the Marble Collegiate Church in New York City. Following the small ceremony, which included the couple's immediate families and a few close friends,

Donald and Ivana Trump stand outside the Federal Courthouse. Ivana was sworn in as an American citizen in May 1988.

Trump and his bride enjoyed an elegant reception at the exclusive 21 Club. The Trumps then honeymooned in exotic Acapulco, Mexico.

Once home from his honeymoon, Trump jumped back into the fray to keep the Commodore project moving forward. That same year, the Trumps welcomed their first child, Donald John Trump, Jr., into the world on December 31. They called him Donny. Construction on the Commodore began in June 1978. With the help of his architect, Der Scutt, Trump was now ready to make his vision for the hotel come to life.

For the exterior of the building he used reflective glass. It immediately updated the hotel's look and made it gleam with flash and glamour. Next, he gutted the building's interior and rebuilt it with 1,400 larger rooms, rather than its previous 2,500 tiny rooms. And finally, he created a spectacular lobby. It was several stories high, and decorated with lush plants and fountains. He also installed a warm brown-colored marble for the floor, along with shiny brass railings and columns. In addition, he built a glass-enclosed restaurant, which projected over Forty-second Street. The renovated hotel was called the Grand Hyatt. It would be one of the few Trump properties that did not bear the Trump name.

The hotel's renovation took over a year. As the project moved forward, Donald Trump established his work habits. Just like his father, Fred, he worked

Trump and his ten-year-old son, Donald Trump, Jr., attend a boxing match at Trump Plaza, June 27, 1988.

constantly. He used travel time in his chauffeur-driven silver Cadillac limousine to catch up on telephone calls. An assistant often rushed papers needing his signature to wherever he might be having lunch. And Trump's lunches were either business related or nonexistent. When he was free for lunch, he might not eat at all, or else he would grab a quick sandwich to eat while he worked. Trump's lifelong high energy and drive kept him going. Even sleep did not slow him down—he could function just fine with very little.[22]

Trump's style with his employees was typically positive and upbeat. Convinced that he only hired the best, he treated his staff well.[23] That is, unless mistakes were made. When that happened, Trump's temper could be ferocious.[24] Yet, his employees knew how hard their boss worked, and that he expected their best efforts. They either gave that or found another company to work for.

Meanwhile, Ivana Trump got involved with New York City's elite social set by volunteering to raise money for charities. She was also responsible for establishing her husband's nickname, "the Donald." Her native Czech language does not require articles, such as "a" and "the" as we do in English. So when speaking English, she often put articles in front of nouns whether they were needed or not. Speaking in her heavily accented English in an interview with *The New York Times*, Ivana said, "The Donald is fantastic in the golf and very good in the tennis."[25] The phrase stuck, and from then on he has often been referred to as "the Donald."

Ivana was also interested in her husband's real-estate business. Once renovation began at the Commodore, she enjoyed visiting the work site, wearing expensive designer dresses and high heels, along with a hard hat. Before long, Trump put his wife in charge of the building's interior design. Not surprisingly, her presence was rather distracting for the construction workers.[26] She was also criticized for interfering with business decisions and being overbearing.[27] But "the Donald" loved that his very capable wife was interested in his work. Not only did he approve of her decorating work, he also saw her on-site presence as giving him an extra set of eyes and ears so he would always know what was going on.[28]

Once the Commodore renovation was completed, the thirty-four-story Grand Hyatt opened in November 1980 with great fanfare. And true to Trump's vision, it was a big success from the first.[29] At the same time, his dream of becoming a recognized and respected "player" in Manhattan real estate was coming true.[30]

5

TOWER OF TREATS

I
n 1982, Trump hosted a ceremony to celebrate the construction of his latest creation in New York City: Trump Tower. It was scheduled to be completed the following year, and it would become, of all his properties, Trump's favorite.[1] Located on Fifth Avenue at Fifty-sixth Street, Trump viewed the location as the best, most profitable in the world.[2] He had long had his eye on the site, but it was occupied by the Bonwit Teller building. It was an eleven-story limestone structure, which housed the Manhattan branch of the well-known and high-end department store. The building had been built in 1929.

As with the Commodore, Trump was not discouraged by the complexities of getting his new tower built on that site. As he later wrote: "I aim very high, and then I just keep pushing . . . . to get what I'm after."[3] Indeed, he would push for years to get his tower built. First, he called Bonwit Teller's owner, Franklin Jarman, offering to buy the building. But he was turned down. After that, he would send a letter or call again every six months or so just to see if Jarman had changed his mind. He had not. Until one day in 1978, Trump read that Genesco, Incorporated, the parent company for Bonwit Teller, was having financial difficulties and was interested in selling some of its properties.

> "I **aim** very **high, and then I just keep pushing . . . . to get what I'm after."**

This time, Trump's offer to buy the building was accepted. Along with the building itself, for twenty-five million dollars the deal also included the lease for the land it was on. About the deal, Trump would later write that ". . . sheer persistence [can be] the difference between success and failure."[4]

Trump knew that buying the Bonwit Teller land lease was not good enough. It meant that the land was just rented; he did not own it. And the lease was due to expire in just twenty-nine years. The last thing Trump needed was to construct a big building on the property, only to risk having it torn down by the landowner when the land lease expired. So his next move was to contact the owner of the land, the Equitable Life Assurance Society, to see if they would sell it. Which they agreed to do. In exchange, Trump gave them half ownership in what would become his new building.

Next, Trump wanted to buy rights to the air space above the building next door, the famous Tiffany and Company jewelry store. He needed that to create the giant-sized building he envisioned.[5] So he met with Tiffany's owner, Walter Hoving, and convinced him to sell Tiffany's air rights for five million dollars. By the end of 1978, Trump had all the land issues resolved for his new building. A *New York Times* article would note, "That Mr. Trump was able to obtain the location . . . is testimony to [his] persistence and to his skills as a negotiator."[6]

At that point, despite all the progress he had made, Trump's work had only begun. Ahead of him lay all the intricate maneuvering through the complexities of New York City's real-estate transactions. Trump knew that for the kind of high-profile skyscraper he wanted to build, he would need lots of variances, or special permissions, from the city.[7]

Once again, Trump hired his Grand Hyatt architect, Der Scutt, to develop a design for the tower. Always aiming high, he told Scutt, "I want to build the most fantastic building in New York."[8]

Scutt sketched dozens of designs for the building's exterior. Trump reviewed them and chose the parts he liked from each. He later wrote: "[W]ithout a unique design, we'd never get approval for a very big building."9

He wanted his new project to be as tall as possible. That would provide more space for condominiums, which would give the Trump Organization maximum profits. In addition, Trump knew that the views of Central Park and the New York City skyline would be critical for getting the condominiums sold at the highest possible prices.10

From the first, Trump and Scutt decided not to go with a straight boxlike skyscraper. The final design for the building was something different—a saw-toothed, or zigzagged design. It was not only unusual, but gave the building twenty-eight sides. Trump was delighted, because each side provided another view of the city. But first, New York's City Planning Commission had to approve the design. And that would not be easy. One problem was that the building Trump proposed— a flashy high-rise—was a drastic departure from the other buildings in that area.11 Most were built of limestone or brick and were around fifty years old. In contrast, Trump wanted his building's exterior to be a smoky gray glass.

In addition, Trump was proposing a new concept—a multiuse building. The first six stories would be an enclosed shopping mall with exclusive retail stores. The next six floors would be office buildings.

And the remaining stories would be constructed as high-end, very expensive, luxury condominiums.

As expected, the city planners objected to the building's design, and the project was at a standstill until two things happened. First, Trump had Scutt prepare a model for the tower that would meet all the Planning Commission's requirements. When they saw it, even they were disappointed and realized it would not be an asset to the city's architecture.[12] Second, the highly respected *New York Times* newspaper's architecture critic, Ada Louise Huxtable, reviewed the Trump-preferred design. In an article entitled "A New York Blockbuster of Superior Design," Huxtable praised the plan for the building, writing: "A great deal of care has . . . been lavished on its design. It is undeniably a dramatically handsome structure."[13] After that, Trump's plan was unanimously approved by the city in 1979. With 263 condominiums, it would be New York City's tallest residential building.

Chase Manhattan Bank agreed to loan Trump two hundred million dollars to build his tower. Trump knew it would be very expensive to build, but he was convinced that the luxury it afforded would quickly attract clients willing and able to pay top dollar for a spectacular place to live. He hired a woman named Barbara Res to manage the tower's construction. He had seen her work on the Grand Hyatt construction crew and was impressed with her ability. He admired her take-charge attitude and lack of intimidation when working with the tough, mostly male construction workers. When Trump hired her, she became the first woman to be put in charge of constructing a skyscraper in New York City.[14]

Demolition of the Bonwit Teller building began on March 15, 1980. The building had been graced with two bas-relief sculptures above the eighth floor. Bas-relief means that the sculptures were attached to the building, but they were raised slightly from its surface. They were considered by some to be valuable, as well as important from an architectural standpoint. A representative from New York City's Metropolitan Museum of Art had contacted Trump about the possibility of saving the sculptures, along with the iron grille work above the entrance to the store. They hoped that Trump would consider donating the artwork to the museum. Trump agreed.

However, by the time the building was being torn down, his demolition crew advised him that the sculptures were very heavy and would be difficult to remove. It would take a lot of extra time and money to get them down without damaging them. The result was that the sculptures were destroyed. Neither was the grille work saved. That created a lot of negative publicity for Trump. But over time, the storm passed.

Trump was rather surprised by all the negative press he received about the sculptures. He later wrote:

"[D]espite what some people may think, I'm not looking to be a bad guy when it isn't absolutely necessary."[15] Still, looking at the bright side, he saw the publicity as free advertising for his new building.

Trump wanted the tower's atrium, or open lobby, to be spectacular. And he got his wish. By this time, he had hired Ivana as executive vice president in charge of interior design for the Trump Organization. As with the Grand Hyatt, she was responsible for the interior decorating decisions for the building. She chose a rare and beautiful peach-colored marble for the atrium's walls and floor. It was very expensive and would require expert marble cutters to handle it. Ivana went to Italy herself to supervise the job of quarrying the marble. That way she could make sure the tones would match. In all, the Trumps imported 240 tons of the special marble for the Trump Tower atrium.

Along with the striking marble, Ivana used highly polished bronze for the atrium's columns and escalators. Lots of live greenery, including flowers, trees, and shrubs, were also added. At the same time, the atrium contained a spectacular eighty-foot-high waterfall, which added to the dramatic effect of the area. Trump saw the elegance and flair of the atrium as a "symbol of the Trump Organization."[16]

Ivana was a perfectionist, and like her husband, she used her incredible energy and stamina to personally ensure that every possible detail in the building's interior was perfect.[17] But just as at the Grand Hyatt, Ivana Trump's presence at the construction site sometimes irritated the other workers. Ivana was considered too bossy by some, and she was seen as often changing her mind or interfering with others' decisions.[18]

Nevertheless, construction moved forward, and Ivana's famous attention to the tiniest details of the interior paid off. The atrium would later receive an architectural award for excellence from the Fifth Avenue Association.

The building's entrance on Fifth Avenue was dramatically oversized, measuring thirty feet wide. Above the doors, "Trump Tower" was prominently displayed in two-foot-high letters in brass. By this time, Trump had become well known enough in New York City to be interesting to the media. And he used his name well to advertise his projects. Later, he explained, "[I]f you are a little different, or a little outrageous, . . . the press is going to write about you."[19] Trump realized that his attention in the media was as good as paid advertisements to get the word out about his buildings. He also believes in the art of exaggeration, writing that it is "a very effective form of promotion."[20] And he used his name liberally.[21] For example, Trump Tower is advertised as being sixty-eight stories tall, while in reality, it only has fifty-eight floors.[22]

Despite all he had accomplished with the Grand Hyatt and Trump Tower projects, Donald Trump was not always warmly accepted by many of the other real-estate developers in the area. They tended to be more conservative and reserved, a style which generally suited their clients. Trump, on the other hand, was young and thought of as brash and too flashy in his appearance and personality.[23] Still, he received grudging respect for his important real-estate successes.[24]

In the middle of all the Trumps' work on the tower, their lives changed again on October 30, 1981, with the birth of their second child, Ivanka Marie. On top of that, Trump also bought and renovated yet

another building, to be called Trump Plaza. Located on Third Avenue, it provided another option for wealthy clients—this time in an apartment cooperative in which the tenants shared part ownership in the building itself.

Ivana once again helped her husband with the Trump Plaza's interior design, as well as with

Trump and ten-year-old Ivanka attend Maybelline's 1991 Look of the Year event at the Plaza Hotel in New York City.

monitoring the construction to make sure the building was completed on time. It would eventually become home to such celebrities as Dick Clark and Martina Navratilova.

The next year the Trumps began scouting the area for a week-end getaway home. They found what they were looking for in nearby Greenwich, Connecticut. The forty-three-year-old red brick home with white shutters was situated on five acres of land. It also had a glassed-in back porch that overlooked the harbor below. Once they bought it, Ivana set to work getting the home renovated and updated for her family.

Trump Tower officially opened in February 1983, with lots of media fanfare. Trump marketed his condominiums to celebrities as well as to wealthy people from foreign countries. Ultimately, his tenants would include talk-show host Johnny Carson, movie director Steven Spielberg, entertainer and pianist Liberace, and singer Paul Anka.

Trump's most powerful selling feature for his condominiums at Trump Tower was the spectacular and unique views they provided of Central Park, the Manhattan skyline, the Statue of Liberty, and the East and Hudson rivers. For maximum views Trump built the apartments with huge windows that ran almost from ceiling to floor. He also charged the highest prices ever for condominiums in the city. Beginning at five million dollars for a one-bedroom, the price tag rose to eleven million for a three-story triplex. "We positioned ourselves as . . . the hottest ticket in town. We were selling fantasy," he would later write.[25]

For the building's atrium, Trump rented space to some of the most prestigious retail stores in the world, including Cartier's, Martha, and Harry Winston. Shoppers at Trump Tower could buy anything from expensive jewelry to fine crystal and valuable antiques.

The building was an immediate success. Its condominiums sold quickly and the spectacular building drew lots of tourists.[26] With the building's taxes, its stores, the condominiums, and the thousands of jobs it provided, Trump Tower became a huge financial bonus for New York City.[27]

Once the tower was completed, Trump and his family moved in as well, taking one of the two triplexes at the top of the building. Ivana had worked hard to make

Trump Tower

their new home especially luxurious. Using lots of marble, gold leaf, and crystal chandeliers, Trump wanted the quality and opulence of his Trump Tower home to equal that of Versailles Palace outside of Paris, France.[28]

Later, he would combine his triplex with the other penthouse triplex in the tower, creating a gigantic home with fifty rooms. The eighty-foot-long living room provides panoramic views of Central Park, and it includes twenty-seven hand-carved marble columns, along with a twelve-foot-high fountain.

Trump also converted space on the twenty-sixth floor of the tower into offices for the Trump Organization, where they remain today. Three walls of his office are floor-to-ceiling glass, providing panoramic views of the city. Ivana took over an office next to her husband's.

With Trump Tower, Donald Trump's long-time dream of owning high-end Manhattan real estate had come true. He made it happen using a combination of vision, determination, and perseverance, along with a bit of luck. He still had many new projects ahead of him, both in and outside the world of Manhattan real estate.

6
THE FAST LANE

After his spectacular successes with the Grand Hyatt and Trump Tower, Donald Trump was riding high. He had proven that he could pull off major, complex real-estate deals in New York City. And he had willingly taken the huge risks involved with each project. Success was sweet. But if he had failed, he would have faced public humiliation and possible financial ruin.

At the same time, Trump was courting, and getting, a lot of media attention, not only in New York City, but across the country. In 1983, articles began to appear about him in national magazines such as *Town and Country*, *Gentlemen's Quarterly*, and *People*.

With two young children, a beautiful wife helping him, and two spectacular homes, Donald Trump seemed to have it all. So, what was next for "the Donald?" As it turned out, more than even he might have imagined.

Shortly after Trump Tower opened, Trump decided to get involved in the world of professional football. The United States Football League, (USFL) organized the previous year, was a struggling league, which played their games in the spring. That way, they would not have to compete for fans against the powerful National Football League's (NFL) annual fall/winter season. In 1983, Trump bought one of the USFL teams, the New Jersey Generals.

But the USFL was having a hard time. Without many nationally recognized players, most of the USFL teams had small fan bases. And that meant the teams were not bringing in much money. By the end of their second season, the league was in serious financial trouble.[1] But with Trump on board as a USFL team owner, he wanted to change all that. First, he thought the league should play in the fall and compete directly against the NFL. Second, he was convinced that if the USFL teams signed nationally known players away from the NFL, that the league's fan base would expand. Ultimately, he hoped that the USFL teams would merge with the NFL. If that happened, the value of his team, the Generals, would skyrocket.[2] But if the USFL was not successful, Trump thought they should file a lawsuit against the NFL, charging that the NFL was a monopoly. A monopoly is a condition in which one company, in this case the NFL, controls an industry, preventing any competition. If the USFL won that case, Trump thought they would get a big cash settlement, which could help them hire more high-profile players and continue on.

Meanwhile, Trump's attention also took him back to real estate—this time in Atlantic City, New Jersey. Just 125 miles from New York City, Atlantic City had become second only to Las Vegas as a center for high-stakes gambling.

Trump knew gambling could be a very profitable business, and he had thought for years that he might want to get involved in it. So he went to Atlantic City to investigate. At the same time he was working on the Grand Hyatt back in New York City, he found property he was interested in on the Atlantic City Boardwalk.

Actually, the land Trump wanted was made up of three separate pieces of property, with a total of thirty different owners. But Trump was not put off by the problems it would take to buy the land. He was ready to move forward to put the deals together.[3]

Before long, Trump had acquired his boardwalk property and had hired his younger brother, Robert, to manage it. But the casino he planned to build there would be delayed for several years because he could not find a bank to loan him the money to build it. Banks were skeptical about loaning money for casinos, viewing them as a high-risk business.

It would take a couple of years, but finally Trump's luck changed. He was contacted by the Holiday Inn hotel chain. They already had a very successful casino, Harrah's, open in Atlantic City. But it was not on the Boardwalk. And Holiday Inn wanted to own a casino/hotel on the Boardwalk, where most of the tourists and gamblers spent their time. So they suggested a partnership with Trump. Holiday Inn would finance the building on Trump's property, and Trump would build it.

The new casino/hotel opened in 1984. It was called Harrah's at Trump Plaza. The opening was a gala event, with an estimated nine thousand people attending. In the meantime, the USFL lawsuit against the NFL was filed in late 1984. The USFL wanted $1.32 billion in damages. After two years in court, the USFL won their suit. But to their dismay, the jury only awarded them one dollar in damages. With dwindling funds and a decreasing fan base, the USFL folded.

Nevertheless, Trump's national media exposure only increased because of his participation with the USFL.[4] For example, in 1984 his picture was on the cover of the *New York Times Magazine*, with an accompanying article entitled: "The Expanding Empire of Donald Trump." Within the lengthy article, the author wrote: "Donald J. Trump is the man of the hour."[5]

And Trump loved the media attention. He knew it promoted not only his properties, but his personal

fame as well.[6] Nineteen eighty-four was also a special
year for the Trumps, with the addition of their third
child, Eric.

As a father, Trump is quick to admit that when his
children were young he was not very comfortable
spending time with them and playing with them.[7] He
left most of the parenting to their mother, Ivana,
whom he often praised as a
wonderful mother. But as his
children have grown older, he
has become more involved with
them. Despite his hectic schedule, he enjoys their frequent
telephone calls.

The next year, Trump was
once again back in Atlantic
City. His activity there was far
from over. His next acquisition
would be property he bought
from the Hilton Hotel
Corporation. When he bought
it in 1985, the property was
already well under construction. Trump was able to buy it

Twelve-year-old Eric Trump smiles
for the camera with his hamster
Cory as he arrives home from
school in 1996.

because the Hilton Corporation had unexpectedly been denied a gambling license by Atlantic City's Casino Control Commission. Without that, the Hilton Corporation could not own or operate a casino there, so they needed to sell their building.

The hotel/casino contained 615 hotel rooms, along with a large casino floor. Trump bought the property for $320 million. Then he finished the construction and named his new property Trump Castle. It opened in June 1985. Trump put his wife, Ivana, in charge of managing it.

For her new job, Ivana would commute several days each week from New York City to Atlantic City in the Trump helicopter. She arrived early each morning, took care of hotel business, and would return to New York City in the evenings to spend time with her children. Ivana proved to be an excellent manager of Trump Castle. Under her leadership, the property became very successful.[8]

Along with his interest in Atlantic City, Trump continued to scout Manhattan for property to buy and develop. Several years earlier, he had added two more buildings to his growing empire. One was an old apartment building at 100 Central Park South. The other was the Barbizon Hotel next door.

Trump's plan was to tear both buildings down and replace them with a luxurious hotel and shops. But he ran into problems with the people living in the apartment building. The main problem was that the building was rent-controlled. That meant that the rent its tenants paid was protected and kept very low by state and city laws. The laws had been put in place years earlier to provide affordable housing in the city. In addition, the apartments at 100 Central Park South were lovely, with high ceilings, large rooms, and magnificent views of Central Park and the city. And because of rent control, the tenants were getting their exquisite homes at bargain prices.

So when the tenants of 100 Central Park South learned of Trump's plans to tear their building down, they were furious. They organized together, hired a lawyer, and filed a lawsuit against him, claiming that he could not tear down their building and force them to find new homes.

Trump, true to his style, fought back for several years. But in 1985, he finally gave in; the building would remain. In addition, he would renovate it, as well as the Barbizon Hotel next door, converting it into luxury condominiums, and renaming it Trump Parc.

Even though his plans for 100 Central Park South did not go as he had planned, Trump turned the outcome into a victory for himself, publicly saying the tenants had helped him. He said he had saved lots of money by simply renovating the buildings, rather than building a new one.[9]

Also in 1985, the Trumps bought the spectacular Mar-a-Lago estate in Palm Beach, Florida. Mar-a-Lago, which means Sea-to-Lake in Spanish, had been built by Marjorie Merriweather Post, heiress to the Post breakfast food fortune. The mansion had taken four years to build, and was completed in 1927. A magnificent estate, it had 118 rooms, including 58 bedrooms, 33 bathrooms, 27 servants' rooms, a movie theater, and a dining room that could seat as many as 50 guests.

Trump bought the Spanish-Mediterranean-style property for five million dollars. He paid an extra three million dollars for the home's furnishings, along with its tableware, which would accommodate up to two hundred guests. The Mar-a-Lago grounds already had a tennis court, and the Trumps would add a swimming pool and a nine-hole golf course. The home became a winter retreat for the family, as well as a special place to entertain friends and business associates. Trump also turned the estate into a private club. With membership fees at $150,000, club members could schedule Mar-a-Lago for their personal use.

At the same time, Trump formed a partnership with Lee Iacocca, chairman of the Chrysler Corporation. Together they bought a condominium complex in Palm Beach, which they named Trump Plaza of the Palm Beaches.

Back in New York City, in the spring of 1986, Trump turned his attention to the Wollman Skating

Rink in Central Park. Built in 1950, the rink was owned by the city, and it was one of the largest outdoor skating rinks in the world. But it had been closed for repairs in 1980. By 1986, after thirteen million dollars and six years, those repairs still were not finished, and the once-popular rink remained closed.

Trump was disgusted with what he considered the city's embarrassing failure to get the rink back up and running again.[10] In May 1986, he offered to take over the renovation at cost, meaning he would make no profit on the project. He knew it would give him a lot of positive publicity in the city, something he craved and enjoyed.

Under Trump's supervision, the rink reopened in November 1986, having come in under budget and ahead of schedule. A sure media hit, Trump arranged for many of the world's most prominent skaters, including Peggy Fleming and Dorothy Hamill, to be at the opening ceremonies. As with the renovation of the Grand Hyatt, Trump came off not only as a great real-estate developer, but also as a hero for New York City.[11] An earlier news article praised him for helping "lead the city out of the darkness of the mid-1970s."[12]

During this time, Ivana and her husband's relationship was taking a downturn. Their competitive natures had become a problem—they had begun to compete against each other.[13] In addition, they enjoyed different things. She loved champagne, fancy meals, and high-society parties. He, on the other hand, had more simple tastes in food, hated the small talk required at parties, and liked to go to bed early.[14]

By 1987, Trump's head was turned by another beautiful blonde, Marla Maples. When they met, she was twenty-three; he was forty. From Dalton, Georgia, she was a beauty pageant winner, a swimsuit model, and an aspiring actress. Unknown to Ivana, Trump and Marla became romantically involved.[15]

Also in 1987, Trump added the world of publishing to his activities by writing, with the help of Tony Schwartz, his first book. He had been approached by Random House publishers to write his autobiography. The resulting book was called *Trump: The Art of the Deal.* It quickly became a best seller.

To celebrate, Trump held what he would call, "The Party of the Year" at Trump Tower. Among the two thousand guests who attended were such celebrities as Barbara Walters and Michael Douglas, along with prominent New York politicians and Trump business associates. In addition, he made the interview circuit, promoting his book on a number of television talk shows.[16]

In the Media

In the 1980s, the Trump name was becoming increasingly familiar to people across the country. More and more articles about "the Donald" were printed in national magazines. Trump also began appearing on talk shows such as *Larry King Live* and *Saturday Night Live*. He was on a roll. A big roll!

Ever on the alert to add to his holdings, in 1987 Trump bought the world's third largest yacht, which he named the *Trump Princess*. It cost him twenty-nine million dollars. The yacht contained eleven ultra-luxury guest suites, each named for a different precious or semiprecious stone. The magnificent yacht also had two waterfalls, a helipad, three elevators, and a three-bed infirmary, along with living quarters for more than fifty servants.

Despite his purchase, Trump was not fond of boating and never spent a night on the luxury yacht.[17] He would later admit, "It makes me nervous to relax."[18] Instead, he used the yacht to entertain clients and high-roller gamblers from his casinos in Atlantic City. At the same time, he started making plans to sell the *Trump Princess* and build an even bigger and more opulent yacht.[19]

The next year, Trump bought the world-famous Plaza Hotel in New York City. Built in 1907, the luxury hotel was located along Central Park South in Manhattan. It had been built to look like a French chateau, or small castle. Considered a New York City landmark, the hotel was also well known as the setting for the famous Eloise children's book series by Kay Thompson. In addition, the building was used as part of the set in a number of movies, including *Home Alone 2: Lost in New York*.

Trump paid approximately four hundred million

dollars for the Plaza. It was a price he knew was too high. But in an article published in *The New York Times*, he explained, "This isn't just a building. It's the ultimate work of art. I was in love with it."[20] After buying the Plaza, Trump transferred Ivana from Trump Castle in Atlantic City back to New York City to manage his latest purchase and oversee its renovation.

The next spring, Trump also expanded into the airline industry. He bought twenty-one Boeing 727 airplanes from Eastern Airlines Shuttle, renaming them Trump Air. After updating and improving the interior of the planes, they became his shuttle service, which carried airline commuters between New York City, Boston, and Washington, D.C.

> **"This isn't just a building. It's the ultimate work of art. I was in love with it."**

That same year, Trump suffered a tremendous business loss when his three top casino executives were killed in a helicopter crash in October. They were on their way to Atlantic City after a meeting with Trump earlier that morning in New York City. He was devastated personally and professionally by the tragedy, later writing: "I felt sadder than I've ever felt in my life."[21]

Despite the tragic loss to the Trump Organization, business continued. Back in Atlantic City, Trump's most spectacular property there would become the

The forty-two-story Trump Taj Mahal Casino Resort brightens up the night sky in Atlantic City.

Trump Taj Mahal hotel/casino. He bought it for a reported $273 million when it was half finished and would spend more than $500 million to complete it. It became one of the world's largest casinos, with 3,000 slot machines and 160 gaming tables. On the downside, the spectacular property needed to take in $1.3 million from its customers each day just to keep the building operating and its employees paid.

The Trump Taj Mahal opened in April 1990, billed as the "'Eighth Wonder of the World.'"[22] The opening night ceremonies were dramatic and spectacular. With hundreds of people attending and lots of publicity, Trump began by rubbing an Aladdin's lamp, after which a genie appeared, followed by a laser show and fireworks.

By 1990, Donald Trump's empire was enormous and diverse. But trouble loomed ahead. It would become almost more than even he could handle.

7

A HOUSE
OF CARDS

A few years after Trump Tower had opened, something happened in the real-estate industry that would nearly destroy Donald Trump and his empire. Real-estate prices tend to go in cycles. Some years the value of property is high, and so its prices are, too. On the other hand, real estate can also sink into a depression, when property values and prices drop.

In the late 1980s and early 1990s, real-estate values dropped across the country. With that, income for Trump's buildings dropped as well. He could no longer charge as much for his luxury condominiums. On top of that, his casino businesses were not bringing in as much money as he needed to cover the payments on the huge bank loans he had taken out to build them.

Trump blamed his casino problems on Atlantic City. First, the city's cold winter weather sent potential gamblers to warmer climates for a large part of each year. And second, he saw the city itself as not very appealing to visitors. Instead, he thought it looked run-down and depressed.1 In addition, with the recent loss of his three top casino executives, Trump's chances of handling his money crisis only worsened.

Suddenly, with dwindling income, Trump could not make his monthly loan payments to the banks. And once that happened, he was in danger of losing his buildings and having the banks take them over. Because of his name and reputation, banks had loaned Trump more than they should have.[2] According to a *New York Times* article in June 1990, the Trump Organization owed more than two billion dollars to various banks.[3] He was very close to bankruptcy.

Trump was certainly not the only real-estate developer facing financial ruin during that time. Many others were as well, and a number of them were forced to declare bankruptcy.[4]

At the same time that Trump's financial world was falling apart, his marriage was, as well. Ivana found out about his ongoing relationship with Marla Maples and filed for divorce.

The Trumps had signed a prenuptial, or before-marriage, agreement stating which Trump assets Ivana would get if she and her husband ever did, indeed, divorce. But by this time, Ivana felt the prenuptial agreement was not fair; that it did not give her enough share of her husband's fortune. She thought she deserved one-half of Trump's wealth, and she was ready to go to court to fight for it.[5]

With all his problems, it was the worst time in Donald Trump's life.[6] But the media attention he had always enjoyed kept right on going. Now, instead of flattering articles about his wealth and talent, the media rushed to print every possible detail they could get about his financial downfall and his marital problems. His status as a public figure, which he had enjoyed for so long, was now working against him. Day by day, he had to endure public humiliation. And he knew lots of people were delighted to see him in trouble.[7] He was also especially distressed by the upsetting effect all the media attention about his separation from Ivana was having on his children.[8]

> "It **never** occurred to me to **give up**, to **admit** defeat."

Nevertheless, Trump's "can-do" spirit, which had gotten him so far, would not fail him in his time of peril. About that time in his life, he later wrote: "It never occurred to me to give up, to admit defeat."[9] Just as he had done with all of his property deals, he was ready to fight.

Trump knew the first thing he needed to do was to

gather his bankers together and try to work out arrangements with them. He needed them either to reduce his loan payments, or refinance his loans at lower interest rates so he would not have to pay so much money each month. Another option was to persuade them to postpone his payments for several years. All these plans, however, would mean that the banks would not get back all the money they had loaned him. So why would they even think of agreeing to his pleas for help? The reason is that if they did not, and Trump did, indeed, file for bankruptcy, all the banks would get would be his buildings, which they did not want, because they would have to sell them at huge losses. The banks would end up with some of their loaned money back, but not nearly as much as they would if they helped Trump, and he were able to get back on his feet financially.[10]

So that is what many of them did. Trump called a meeting of representatives from ninety banks from around the world that had loaned him money. They met in his conference room at Trump Tower or attended by conference call. Of that meeting, he would later write: "I will never forget the day I was forced to call the banks to renegotiate my loans. This was something that I never thought could happen to me."[11]

Trump explained his situation to the bankers, asked for their help, and clearly pointed out the advantage it would be for them if they helped him instead of cutting him loose. He later wrote about that meeting: "That was the biggest bet of my life, and boy, did it pay off!"[12]

Many banks agreed to work with him, easing his immediate debt by at least sixty-five million dollars, and delaying payments on much of the rest.[13] Some banks, on the other hand, refused to negotiate a deal with him. Trump would never forget or forgive those banks that chose not to help him.[14]

Trump also fought back with the press, always appearing upbeat and proclaiming that his difficulties would work out over time.[15] Looking back and trying to learn from his problems, Trump admitted, "I got caught up in the buying frenzy."[16] He also realized that he was "too competitive for [his] own good."[17]

In the meantime, to get more cash Trump sold his most unprofitable holdings, including Trump Plaza of the Palm Beaches; his yacht, the *Trump Princess*; and his airline shuttle service. He also turned to his family for help. His father, Fred, helped him with a multimillion dollar loan. He also borrowed millions of dollars from his siblings.[18] By the time Trump was through fighting for his business, he was still financially alive. Even so, he would have to continue to juggle funds carefully for the next several years to stay afloat.

In 1990, Trump published his second book, *Trump: Surviving at the Top*, with the help of writer

Charles Leerhsen. As with his first book, this one also became a *New York Times* best seller.

Trump's divorce from Ivana was granted in late 1990. She gave up her lawsuit and ended up settling for the terms in the prenuptial agreement. With that, in 1991, she received $10 million in cash, their Greenwich, Connecticut, home, $100,000 each year in child support for each of their three children, $350,000 each year for alimony, and a $4 million housing allowance.[19] Despite their divorce, Trump continues to claim that he will always love Ivana.[20]

Meanwhile, Trump's relationship with Marla Maples moved forward. In October 1993, they had their first and only child together, a daughter whom they named Tiffany Ariana. Two months later they were married at the Plaza Hotel, with more than one thousand guests attending the ceremony.

Meanwhile, Trump had long been working on yet another new development. This would be at the West Side rail yard at Sixtieth Street along the Hudson River. It had long been one of the most valuable undeveloped pieces of property left in Manhattan.

Trump had wanted to build on this property since his career in Manhattan began years earlier. But without city support, his development proposals fell flat, and he ended up letting his option on the property lapse. Nevertheless, he had bought it back again in 1985, and he had been fighting with the city and

Marla Maples and Donald Trump leave the hospital with their newborn daughter Tiffany.

community groups about plans for the property ever since.

In typical fashion, Trump planned for a massive development of the West Side rail yard. Along with up to seven thousand apartments in six, seventy-story buildings, he also wanted to include business offices and a big shopping mall on the property. On top of that, Trump wanted the area to include the world's tallest building. He was convinced that such a building should be in New York City, rather than in Chicago, where the Sears Tower claimed the title at that time.

Trump also knew that the NBC television studios, located in New York City's Rockefeller Center, were considering moving to a less expensive location. He wanted to entice them to move to his West Side development. To encourage them, he planned to build television and movie studios as part of the complex. He wanted to call the development Television City.

Just as with his earlier attempts to develop the property, Trump ran into immediate opposition from the city, as well as from many of the home-owners in the surrounding neighborhoods. They formed a group called Westside Pride to work against him. They campaigned to the city officials that Trump's proposed project would be bad for the area. They complained that with so many new residents in the area, it would create massive traffic problems and overcrowded schools. Neither did they want high-rise apartment buildings there.[21]

After years of battle with the city and neighborhood opposition, all the affected groups finally came up with a compromise plan. It would not include the world's tallest building; nor would it be home to NBC, which remained at Rockefeller Center. Instead, the development, to be called Riverside South, would include fewer apartments than Trump had originally proposed. The final plan allowed for up to 5,700 units in 16 high-rise buildings. In addition, Riverside South would include a twenty-three-acre public park along the Hudson River. The new plan was approved by the city in late 1992.[22]

Trump later sold the land to a group of Hong Kong investors. Still, he maintained a high profile with the project, as the investors hired him to build and manage the development. It is scheduled to be completed in 2008, and Trump's name will still be prominently displayed on the buildings. Along with Riverside South, the project is also often referred to as Trump Place. About the project, Trump later wrote: "Some things are worth waiting for. . . . This could prove to be my finest contribution to the city of New York."[23]

Slowly, by the mid-1990s, Trump began to pull back from the brink of financial disaster. At the same time, the real-estate industry was beginning to come out of its slump.[24] Trump would later write about his close call with financial ruin with the words, "My policy is to learn from the past, focus on the present, and dream about the future."[25]

8

COMEBACK

By the mid-1990s, Trump's extreme financial problems were finally coming under control. With all his hard work and successful negotiating, along with an upturn in the country's economy, he was standing on firmer financial ground.

The next ten years would bring many more changes to Donald Trump's busy life. In 1994 his father—long his business partner and advocate—died from pneumonia. Fred had also suffered from Alzheimer's disease. He was ninety-three years old when he died. Despite his advanced age, Fred had never retired, each day going to his office on Avenue Z in the Bronx in a chauffeur-driven limousine. His wife, Mary, continued living in the Trump family home in Queens.

Donald had remained close to his father throughout

his life. He would later write: "I learned to think like a billionaire by watching my father, Fred Trump. He was the greatest man I'll ever know, and the biggest influence on my life."[1] And Fred had always stood by his son, through good times and bad. Even during his son's most difficult financial times, Fred supported him, saying, "Don't worry about Donald, I've watched him all of his life. Donald is a winner and will have no troubles."[2]

Despite his father's death, Trump moved his organization forward. In 1994, his next project took him to a building on the southwest corner of Central Park. Built in 1969, the outdated, fifty-two-story building was owned by the General Electric Investment Corporation. Trump wanted to buy it, gut it, and strip the building's exterior down to its steel frame. Then he would reconstruct it into a building that would contain a combination of luxury hotel rooms and condominiums.

Construction began in 1995. When completed, the new structure contained 264 condominiums and 164 hotel suites. Trump also added a highly rated restaurant, called Jean-Georges, in the building. Trump called his newest creation the Trump International Hotel and Tower.

Throughout his career, Trump always looked forward to his next project. In fact, he said he liked to have at least ten business deals going at the same time.[3]

An executive one-bedroom city suite in the Trump International Hotel and Tower.

As he would write: "To be always moving toward a new goal . . . [is] as close to happiness as you're going to get in life."[4]

Even so, part of the Trump Organization was not always moving forward. By 1995, despite his earlier loan restructuring, Trump's Atlantic City hotel/casinos were still not making enough money to cover the loan payments he had to make on them. To get more cash, Trump pulled his Atlantic City properties together and formed a publicly held company called Trump Hotels and Casino Resorts. That meant that he could raise much-needed money by selling stock, or shares of ownership, in the newly formed company. The downside for Trump was that he would be responsible to his stockholders and a board of directors. They could vote to disapprove of his decisions and leadership. It put him in an uneasy position, which he was not used to and did not like.

Up until this time, as president and chief executive officer (CEO) of the Trump Organization, Trump was solely in charge of all his properties. And he liked it that way, because he made all the company decisions and was responsible for explaining them to no one but himself. Yet at this point, he saw the option of making his casinos a public company as a necessary evil. Looking to keep his Atlantic City properties up and running, Trump said in an interview, "I've never had partners, and I don't want them now. But I could make a lot of money. . . . It's a great opportunity."[5]

In 1996, Trump turned his attention to an old, vacant office building at 40 Wall Street in Manhattan. With seventy stories, at the time it was built it had been second only to the Empire State Building in height. But over time, the once-grand office building in the heart of Manhattan's financial district had become

> "To be always moving toward a new goal . . . [is] as close to happiness as you're going to get in life."

run-down. Trump, however, recognized the value of the property, with its prime location and its spectacular views.[6] He wanted to turn it back into a "first-class office building."[7]

So he bought the building and gutted it from top to bottom. Then he rebuilt its interior into beautiful new offices. He also added an elegant lobby on the ground floor, spending an estimated two hundred million dollars on the project. When he was finished, he named the renovated building the Trump Building at 40 Wall Street. Always proud of his work, Trump considered it one of the best deals he ever made,[8] and "the most beautiful building in lower Manhattan."[9]

Trump had claimed for years that his name on a building added to its value. In one of his books he wrote: "Trump has become a great brand name, due to my rigorous standards of design and quality."[10] And his 40 Wall Street building would be no exception. Its offices were quickly rented, and the building became another big success for Trump.[11]

That same year, Trump partnered with CBS to own and broadcast the three largest beauty competitions in the world: *Miss Universe*, *Miss USA*, and *Miss Teen USA*. Later he changed networks, going with NBC instead, as CBS did not promote the pageants as aggressively as he wanted.

In 1997, Trump's third book, *Trump: The Art of the Comeback*, appeared in bookstores. Writer Kate

Bohner helped him put the book together. It would be his third best seller. As for his very successful venture into the publishing world, Trump would write: "I like writing books, and if I like something, I can find the time for it!"[12]

Meanwhile, Trump and his second wife, Marla, had a long and stormy relationship. About the problems in their marriage, he later wrote: "Sadly . . . we just drifted apart. Our lifestyles became less and less compatible."[13] Still, she had stuck by him during his darkest years, when his business empire and marriage to Ivana were falling apart. But by 1997, the couple separated, finally divorcing in 1999. Trump gave her one million dollars along with generous ongoing child support for their daughter, Tiffany.

Around that time, Trump met the woman who became his new love interest—Melania Knauss. Born in Slovenia (then part of the former Soviet Republic of Yugoslavia), she was twenty-four years younger than he. A stunning brunette, she was modeling in the United States for a fashion event when they met.

Their relationship took off from the start. Trump would later describe Melania as "just as beautiful on the inside as she is on the outside."[14] She also had a calming influence on his hectic life, and he felt lucky to be with her.[15] Before long, she moved into Trump Tower with him.

The next year, Trump continued his successful run

Donald Trump and fashion model Melania Knauss attend an NBC event in New York City, 2004.

in the publishing world by writing his fourth book, *The America We Deserve.* He wrote it because he was concerned that America was seen as weak by other countries, such as Japan and Germany.[16]

Trump also candidly described what he saw as problems in the United States—government bureaucracy, the public-school system, and crime. According to one book description, "Throughout [the book] Trump points out problems and offers sensible, practical solutions."[17]

At the same time, Trump was considering the possibility of running for U.S. president. Eventually, he decided against it, realizing that he was too outspoken to be successful in politics. And besides, he already loved the job he had.[18]

Trump's next construction project would be known as Trump World Tower at United Nations Plaza. Located near the United Nations building on the East Side of Manhattan, with seventy stories,

Trump claimed his new structure would be the world's tallest residential building.[19]

As with all Trump's buildings, luxury was his first priority. It would contain one-, two-, and three-bedroom condominiums. In addition, it offered four-bedroom penthouses, which included maid's quarters and wood-burning fireplaces, along with incredible views of the city. The building also had a health club, a sixty-foot swimming pool, and a top-rated restaurant.

Over the next few years, along with constructing buildings, Trump turned his attention to his other passion—golf.[20] He had begun playing when he was eighteen years old, and he considered it a great way to get business accomplished. He wrote: "Playing golf with a business associate . . . is seldom a waste of time."[21] In fact, in his book, *Trump: The Art of the Comeback*, he lists "Play Golf" as his number one comeback tip.

In 2001, Trump's first golf club opened in Florida. Located in West Palm Beach, it was called the Trump International Golf Club. As with his buildings, Trump planned to create the best golf course in the world. He spent forty million dollars creating a world-class, eighteen-hole golf course. The landscaping was spectacular, with tropical plants and trees, waterfalls, and meandering streams throughout. In addition, the course was graced with a magnificent

Mediterranean-style clubhouse. Memberships at the exclusive golf club were set at $250,000.[22] The next year, Trump's West Palm Beach Golf Club received a Five Star Diamond Award as the best golf course in Florida.

Trump would continue to expand his golf club holdings. One became the Trump National Golf Club, Westchester, located just thirty minutes from Manhattan. He also bought what would become the Trump National Golf Club, Bedminster, in Bedminster, New Jersey. It was already a world-class, eighteen-hole golf course on 525 acres of rolling New Jersey countryside. The clubhouse is an elegant restored mansion built in 1939. Along with golf, the club also offers miles of horseback-riding trails, tennis courts, and several guest cottages.

In 2002, Trump bought the Ocean Trails Golf Course in Los Angeles, California. The three-hundred-acre course extends along the Pacific coast, offering panoramic ocean views from each of its eighteen holes. Trump renovated the course and upgraded it to his standards.[23]

Also that year, Trump bought yet another building in Manhattan—the former Hotel Delmonico. Built in 1929, the property was located at Park Avenue and East Fifty-ninth Street. He turned it into thirty-five stories of luxury condominiums. The building was completed in 2004 and became known as Trump Park Avenue.

At the same time, Trump's casino properties were once again in financial trouble. They still were not making enough money to show a profit. Without that, Trump was unable to keep up with the maintenance they needed or to make improvements to be competitive with other Atlantic City casinos.

So in October 2004, Trump faced his Atlantic City financial problems by restructuring his hotel/casino debt with the banks he owed money to, just as he had done years earlier. Within a year, the company was on steadier footing financially, and it had pulled away from bankruptcy with a new name: Trump Entertainment Resorts Holdings. As part of that transaction, Trump gave up his title as chief executive officer, but remained the company's chairman of the board.

Still, after all he had accomplished, new adventures and even greater fame lay ahead for "the Donald."

The Price of Fame

By 2004, the Trump name was recognized throughout the United States.[24] And in New York City, where he would often walk from Trump Tower to inspect his nearby properties, he was forced to hire a bodyguard to accompany him because of the stir his presence caused among people on the streets. Many wanted his autograph. Some just wanted to touch him, hoping his flair for making money would rub off on them.[25]

9

A NEW CAREER

One day in 2002, Trump got a telephone call from a television producer named Mark Burnett. Although the two men had never met, Trump needed no introduction to Burnett. The British-born entrepreneur had made a huge name for himself in the United States as the creator of the popular reality game show, *Survivor*. He was calling Trump to see if he could film the final episode of *Survivor's* fifth season at Wollman Skating Rink in Central Park.

Trump agreed, and on the day the filming took place, Trump strolled over to make sure everything was going to Burnett's satisfaction. When he got there, he was astonished to see how the television crew had transformed the skating rink. They had made it look like a jungle to match *Survivor's* seasonal setting in Thailand.

While there, he met Burnett, who asked to meet with Trump the following week.

Survivor had first aired in the United States on CBS in 2000. Burnett got the idea for the show from a similar one that had become quite popular in England, and he had persuaded CBS to try an American version. In *Survivor*, which takes place in remote areas all over the world, contestants are divided into tribes. Each week they are pitted against each other to perform a variety of tasks, or "challenges."

Survivor would make television history. It became the first profitable and highly rated of what would become something new to television: the reality show. With its success, *Survivor* was quickly followed by many other reality shows such as *The Bachelor*, *American Idol*, and *Fear Factor*.

Many reality shows have failed to attract a large following and have been canceled after a short run. But popular or not, they are relatively inexpensive to produce. When a television network scores a hit reality show, it can be extremely profitable for them.

Ever in search of a new idea for another hit reality show, Burnett met with Trump in New York to discuss his latest idea—a reality show based in the business world. Rather than set in a jungle like *Survivor*, Burnett's vision was for the new show to take place in the "concrete jungle" of New York City. He had read Trump's book, *Trump: The Art of the Deal*, years earlier when he was new to the United States and making a living selling T-shirts in California. He told Trump the book had changed his life. Now he wanted to work with Trump to try a reality show with a business theme.

He thought the show would be "educational" for its viewers, later writing, "People would be able to see how the real business world works and what it takes to survive in it."[1]

At the same time, Jeff Zucker, president of NBC Entertainment, needed to find a replacement for the popular television show, *Friends*. A long-running situation comedy, *Friends* would be ending a ten-year run on television, during which it had gained tens of millions of fans. With the show going off the air in 2004, it would leave a big hole in Thursday night television on NBC.

Although Zucker thought Burnett's concept with Trump had potential, there was some concern that people outside New York City would not find the show interesting.[2] But Zucker remained positive, saying, "I knew that Donald was universal. He's been up, he's been down, he's been back up again."[3]

With agreement on the show finalized between Trump,

How It Began

This was not the first time Trump had been approached about participating in reality television. But others' ideas had centered around filming his daily activities, and he was not interested. He said he could not do business with film cameras in his face all the time. But Burnett's idea was different: a thirteen-week-job interview with Mr. Trump. The idea captured Trump's interest.

Burnett, and NBC, word was sent out to talent agents in major cities across the country to find applicants for the show. They advertised for "young business professionals looking to get a leg up in their careers."[4] Two hundred and fifteen thousand eager applicants responded. Each produced a ten-minute audition tape, along with a twelve-page application. That group was cut to eleven thousand, who were granted in-person interviews. The remaining fifty semifinalists were sent to Los Angeles to have a personal interview with Mark Burnett. He made the final selection of sixteen.

Still, according to Bill Rancic, the final winner of *The Apprentice*, Season One, he had no idea what he was really getting into when Burnett picked him for the show. As he prepared for an uncertain amount of time filming in New York City, he later wrote that "it was tough for me to understand what was going on, or what I might or might not be getting myself into."[5] Yet he was willing to take the risk to get some "face time" with the man he considered to be the ultimate entrepreneur, Donald Trump.[6]

Shooting for the first season took seven weeks. During that time, the contestants lived together in a luxurious eight-bedroom condominium in Trump Tower. Assisting Trump each week in deciding who would be fired were two of his top executives, George H. Ross and Carolyn Kepcher.

Once filming began, Trump was astonished with

the amount of time it took from his already hectic schedule. Burnett had predicted it would cost Trump no more than three hours of his time each week. In reality, it took ten times that much. Nevertheless, Trump enjoyed working on the show. He especially loved the drama he added to the episodes when he entered the boardroom.[7] And he had no lines to learn or acting to do. His job was to be himself, and the dialogue was completely unscripted.

Trump also enjoyed getting to know the show's job candidates, later writing: "The sixteen applicants quickly became people I liked and cared about. . . . It wasn't easy to fire any of them."[8] On top of everything, Trump was delighted with the attention the show gave him and the Trump Organization. He saw it as free publicity and advertising.[9]

The concept of a thirteen-week interview proved to make for very successful reality television. It aired from January through April 2004. Trump took the title of executive producer for the show as well as host, and he was paid $50,000 per episode. NBC pays the season's winner their $250,000 salary when they go to work for Trump. During that first

> **"The sixteen applicants quickly became people I liked and cared about. . . . It wasn't easy to fire any of them."**

season an average of twenty million people watched each episode.

Trump has made it clear that he thinks he is a big reason for the show's success. He does not hesitate to mention that a similar show with Martha Stewart only lasted one season. The reason? According to Trump, Stewart did not have the personality or charisma needed to keep viewers coming back. He would later say in an interview, "How do you think *The Apprentice* would have done if I wasn't a part of it? There are a lot of imitators now and we'll see how they'll do, but I think they'll crash and burn."[10]

On casting Trump, Burnett seemed to agree with his assessment, saying, "I knew clearly that there was only one master who was colorful enough, charismatic enough, who is really a billionaire, [that] was Trump."[11] And perhaps he is right.

After the success of the first season, Trump negotiated with NBC for a higher salary for the second season. He used the *Friends'* cast salaries to make his point in asking for $18 million per episode. He did not get that, but according to Trump, he got "substantially more" than $1.25 million per episode.[12]

Despite the first season's success of *The Apprentice*, fewer television viewers watched the show's second season. Some thought it was because the cast members were not as interesting and entertaining as they had been in the first season.[13] Even so, the second season's finale drew an impressive sixteen million viewers.

At the same time, the show's episodes became part of business curriculum at some universities. Students would view them and discuss the business ethics and tactics used in each week's task.

The show has also had an effect on people's view of Trump. As he would admit, "I think that people learned that I'm a nicer person when I did *The Apprentice*."[14]

The year 2004 was an eventful one for Donald Trump. In addition to *The Apprentice* debut, he also released two more books. One was written with the help of Meredith McIver and called *Trump: How to Get Rich*. According to one review: "Trump's books have done an effective job of capturing his grand personality in print, and this volume is no exception."[15] Trump's other book that year was *Trump: The Way to the Top: The Best Business Advice I Ever Received*. It contains business advice he gathered from more than one hundred other successful business people.

The Apprentice successfully continued, with the sixth season taking place in Los Angeles, California, rather than New York City. For seasons five and six, Trump also used winning project managers, former *Apprentice* winners, his daughter Ivanka, and his son Donald, Jr., as his advisers, instead of George Ross and Carolyn Kepcher. Season seven aired in January 2008, this time with celebrities as candidates, vying for the title of Trump's "Best Business Brain."

As winner of *The Apprentice's* first season, Bill Rancic's prize was to help manage one of Trump's in-process projects: Trump International Hotel and Tower, Chicago. Located in downtown Chicago, Illinois, the massive building is scheduled for completion by 2009. Once finished, it will be the second tallest building in the United States, with ninety-six stories of high-end condominiums, along with hotel guest rooms and suites. The building will also contain a health club and spa, exclusive retail shops, and fine restau-

Three contestants from the sixth season of *The Apprentice* face "the Donald."

rants. And according to Trump, it will hold the title as the world's tallest residential building. The cost for the building is estimated at more than eight hundred million dollars.

By 2005, in addition to his golf courses and hotel/casinos, Trump had eleven buildings in Manhattan with his name on them. While some may criticize that as being egotistical, still, he insists it assures his clients of the high quality they can expect from him.[16] And he has no intention of discontinuing the practice.

The Trump International Hotel and Tower in Chicago under construction. It is expected to be ready for business in 2009.

10
NEW HORIZONS

With the success of *The Apprentice*, Donald Trump's life only got busier— his real-estate deals never missed a beat, and his empire just continued to expand. He also released yet another book in 2005, called *Trump: The Best Golf Advice I Ever Received.*

At the same time, his family also continued to expand. Trump and his love of six years, Melania Knauss, were married on January 22, 2005. The couple had become engaged earlier, after he had given her a thirteen-carat diamond engagement ring costing an estimated $1.5 million. They were married in the Bethesda-by-the-Sea Episcopal Church in Palm Beach, Florida. About 450 guests, including a number of celebrities, attended. Melania wore a Christian Dior wedding gown made of more than one hundred hand-beaded yards of ivory-colored silk.

The guests were then treated to an extraordinary reception in Mar-a-Lago's grand ballroom. With decorations of white and gold, more than ten thousand white flowers of every kind were used to adorn the room. Chef Jean-Georges Vongerichten flew in from New York City to prepare an elegant dinner for the guests.[1]

In 2006, Trump's next book, *Why We Want You to be Rich: Two Men—One Message*, was published. He wrote it in partnership with another well-known entrepreneur, Robert T. Kiyosaki, along with Meredith McIver and Sharon Lechter. *Publisher's Weekly* reviewed the book, writing: "[T]his collaboration of real estate magnate and rags-to-riches financial guru manages to entertain and to inform."[2]

Also that year, Trump's first child with Melania, Barron William Trump, was born. Meanwhile, Trump's other children had grown up. All three of his children with Ivana work for the Trump Organization as vice presidents of real-estate acquisition and development. Donald, Jr., married. He and his wife had their first child in the summer of 2007, making Donald Trump a grandfather. As of 2008, Trump's daughter with Marla Maples, Tiffany, was living in California with her mother.

Donald Trump's life seems to be exactly as he

Trump talks about his Trump International Hotel and Tower in Chicago during a news conference in May 2007 while his three adult children (Donald Jr., Eric, and Ivanka, left to right) look on. All three of them work for the Trump Organization as vice presidents of real-estate acquisition and development.

would like it. And despite his ever-increasing number of projects, he shows no signs of slowing down. Quite to the contrary, his real-estate projects only continue to mount.

But Trump has not stopped with real estate. In addition to his television career and book collection, he has also established Trump University. It offers online and correspondence classes in such topics as marketing, real estate, and entrepreneurship. Because it is not an accredited university, it cannot grant college credits or

Trump Around the World

In addition to his properties in New York, New Jersey, California, Illinois, and Florida, Donald Trump has spectacular new construction moving forward in Hawaii, Nevada, Georgia, and Louisiana. Trump has also turned his attention outside the United States, with more buildings in process in the Dominican Republic, Korea, Canada, Panama, Brazil, Mexico, and Dubai. Most of these projects will bear Trump's name, even though he will not own them himself. Other developers, recognizing the value of the Trump name, pay him to use it on their buildings.

degrees. Still, it offers opportunities for rising business people to learn how to become more successful. As part of Trump University, Trump released a series of books in 2006, including *Trump University Real Estate 101: Building Wealth With Real Estate Investments*, with Gary W. Eldred; *Trump University Marketing 101: How to Use the Most Powerful Ideas in Marketing to Get More Customers*, with Don Sexton; and *Trump 101: The Way to Success*, with Meredith McIver. The next year he added to the collection with *Trump University Entrepreneurship 101: How to Turn Your Idea Into a Money Machine*, with Michael E. Gordon; and *Trump University Wealth Building 101: Your First 90 Days on the Path to Prosperity*.

He also has a signature collection of Trump products, including men's clothing, leather goods, luggage, eyeglasses, watches, and bottled water. In addition, he has branched out into other product offerings, including

This artist rendering shows the Trump International Hotel and Tower Waikiki Beach Walk in Hawaii scheduled to be completed in 2009. Six-million-dollar condominiums are available for purchase.

Trump Art, Trump Steaks, and the Trump Home Collection, which sells furniture, rugs, home-decorating items, and lighting fixtures. He offers a travel service through GoTrump.com, as well as a home-lending service called Trump Mortgage. He also has a production company in Los Angeles, called Trump Productions.[3] Trump products are readily available from online sources, along with the Trump Store in Trump Tower at 725 Fifth Avenue, New York City.

Trump has always taken a lot of kidding about his hair. And he good-naturedly laughs right along. His hair got more attention than ever once he appeared on *The Apprentice.* But he likes his hair.[4] He admits it might not be his strongest asset, but he has written: "I've been combing (my hair) this way for a long time and I might as well keep doing it."⁵ He emphatically denies that he wears a wig, writing: "My hair is one hundred percent mine."⁶

Throughout his career Trump has had a loyal and very capable assistant working by his side—Norma Foerderer. He hired her early in his career, and through the years she has held the position of gatekeeper to his office and manager of his schedule. She also is the one who decides which, of the hundreds of telephone calls he receives each week, get through to her boss.

Trump has established a reputation for hiring very capable women for high positions in the Trump Organization. He thinks that women work harder to prove themselves.⁷ He explained his philosophy this way: "I'm not a crusader for feminism, I'm not against it, either. I'm just oblivious to a person's gender when it comes to hiring people and handing out assignments."⁸ He is also known for promoting a number of his employees from lower jobs with little experience to positions of high responsibility, based on his instincts about their capabilities.⁹

At the same time, Trump has no respect for weakness in people. He views weakness as not being able to stand up for yourself or to express an opinion with confidence. Rather, he thinks people should not be worried about offending others and should be ready to take on opposition directly.¹⁰ "Toughness is pride, drive, commitment, and the courage to follow through on things you believe in, even when they are under attack," he has written. "It is solving problems instead of letting them fester. It is being who you really are, even when society wants you to be somebody else."[11]

Trump has always had a very short attention span to complement his high energy level.[12] Answering up to one hundred telephone calls every day, each must be quick and to the point. He has no patience for anyone who takes up much of his time.

He is also well known for being a germophobe, or a person with an unusually high fear of germs.[13] He washes his hands frequently and is very uncomfortable with the common business practice of shaking hands. As he said in an interview, "I think shaking hands is barbaric."[14] Rather, he prefers the Japanese practice of a simple short bow to greet others and show respect.[15]

Donald Trump has long been involved in a number of charitable causes. He is on the board of directors for the Police Athletic League and United Cerebral Palsy. He is also chairman of the Donald J. Trump Foundation, and was instrumental in building the New York Vietnam Veterans' Memorial.

He has also been a popular guest on a variety of talk and comedy shows, including *Larry King Live, Saturday Night Live, Late Night With David Letterman,* and *The Tonight Show With Jay Leno.* He has frequently promoted other companies' products, such as Pizza Hut and Visa, on television commercials, and he charges $250,000 as his speaking fee. He had a star in his name added to the Hollywood Walk of Fame in front of the Kodak Theater in 2007.

All the while, Trump's wealth has continued to grow. In late 2006, *Forbes* magazine estimated it to be close to $3 billion.[16]

Throughout his life, Trump has been criticized and made fun of, as well as praised and almost wor-shipped. Some see him as a cutthroat businessman who enjoys destroying his competition. Still others see him as outrageous and bigger than life. As one person put it, "Donald is a

Donald Trump receives his star on the Hollywood Walk of Fame accompanied by his oldest son Donald Trump, Jr., wife Melania, and infant son Barron.

character, a genuine New York character."[17] But no matter what opinion you may have of the man, there is no denying that he has made his mark on American society.

So, what new challenges and adventures lie ahead for Donald Trump? As he himself has answered, "Fortunately, I don't know the answer, because if I did, that would take half the fun out of it."[18]

Ever the optimist, Trump sees his life this way, writing: "With the parents I had and this country as my backbone, anything was possible. I operated on that premise of possibility, and I'm walking, talking proof of the American Dream. For me the American Dream is not just a dream; it's a reality."[19] And based on his past performance, he will continue to make his dreams come true.

> **"For me the American Dream is not just a dream; it's a reality."**

CHRONOLOGY

1946 Donald John Trump is born in Queens, New York, on June 14.

1964 Graduates from New York Military Academy.

1968 Graduates from the University of Pennsylvania Wharton School of Finance.

1971 Moves to studio apartment in Manhattan, New York.

1972 Finalizes first multimillion dollar real-estate transaction with the sale of Swifton Village in Cincinnati, Ohio.

1974 Obtains the option to buy two rail yards in New York City; buys the Commodore Hotel.

1977 Marries Ivana Marie Zelnickova Winklmayr; first child, Donald John Trump, Jr., is born.

1980 Completes the renovation of the Commodore Hotel, which is renamed the Grand Hyatt; begins construction on Trump Tower.

1981 Buys Trump Plaza in New York City; second child, Ivanka Marie, is born.

1982 Buys weekend estate in Greenwich, Connecticut.

1983	Completes construction on Trump Tower; buys USFL New Jersey Generals.
1984	Opens Harrah's at Trump Plaza casino/hotel in Atlantic City, New Jersey; third child, Eric, is born.
1985	Buys Mar-a-Lago estate in Palm Beach, Florida; opens Trump Castle casino/hotel in Atlantic City, New Jersey; renovates the Barbizon Hotel and 100 Central Park South; buys Trump Plaza of the Palm Beaches.
1986	Renovates and reopens the Wollman Skating Rink in Central Park.
1987	Publishes *Trump: The Art of the Deal*, which becomes a *New York Times* best seller; buys yacht, the *Trump Princess*.
1988	Buys the Plaza Hotel in New York City.
1989	Buys fleet of Boeing 727 airplanes to form Trump Air shuttle service; helicopter crash kills three Trump casino executives.
1990	Opens the Trump Taj Mahal casino in Atlantic City, New Jersey; publishes second book, *Trump: Surviving at the Top*; divorces Ivana Trump.
1992	Gains approval for Riverside South development at West Side rail yards.

1993	First child with Marla Maples, Tiffany Ariana, is born; marries Marla Maples.
1995	Creates public company, Trump Hotels and Casino Resorts, for his hotel/casinos in Atlantic City.
1996	Renovates 40 Wall Street to become the Trump Building at 40 Wall Street; completes Trump International Hotel and Tower, Manhattan.
1997	Publishes third book, *Trump: The Art of the Comeback.*
1999	Divorces second wife, Marla Maples.
2000	Publishes fourth book, *The America We Deserve.*
2002	Renovates Hotel Demonico to become Trump Park Avenue.
2004	The first season of *The Apprentice* airs on NBC television; publishes fifth book, *Trump: How to Get Rich*; sixth book, *Trump: The Way to the Top: The Best Business Advice I Ever Received*; and seventh book, *Trump: Think Like a Billionaire: Everything You Need to Know About Success, Real Estate, and Life.*
2005	Marries third wife, Melania Knauss; Atlantic City hotel/casinos emerge from bankruptcy, creating Trump Entertainment Resorts

Holdings; begins construction of Trump International Hotel and Tower in Chicago; publishes eighth book, *Trump: The Best Golf Advice I Ever Received.*

2006 Fifth child, Barron William, is born; publishes series of three books for Trump University; publishes *Why We Want You to be Rich: Two Men—One Message*, with Robert T. Kiyosaki.

2007 Publishes two more books for Trump University; has star with his name installed at the Hollywood Walk of Fame at the Kodak Theater in Los Angeles, California.

CHAPTER NOTES

Chapter 1. "You're Fired!"

1. Bill Rancic, *You're Hired: How to Succeed in Business and Life* (New York: Harper Business, 2004), p. 151.

2. Donald J. Trump, with Meredith McIver, *Trump: How to Get Rich* (New York: Random House, 2004), p. 51.

3. William E. Geist, "The Expanding Empire of Donald Trump," *The New York Times Magazine*, April 8, 1984, p. 28.

4. Donald J. Trump, with Charles Leerhsen, *Trump: Surviving at the Top* (New York: Random House, 1990), p. 41.

5. Robert Slater, *No Such Thing as Over-Exposure: Inside the Life and Celebrity of Donald Trump* (Upper Saddle, N. J.: Pearson Education, Inc., 2005), p. 177.

6. Ibid.

Chapter 2. A Born Competitor

1. Donald J. Trump, with Kate Bohner, *Trump: The Art of the Comeback* (New York: Random House, 1997), p. 116.

2. Donald J. Trump, with Tony Schwartz, *Trump: The Art of the Deal* (New York: Random House, 1987), pp. 47–48.

3. Gwenda Blair, *Donald Trump: Master Apprentice* (New York: Simon & Schuster, 2005), p. 14.

4. Timothy L. O'Brien, *TrumpNation: The Art of Being*

The Donald (New York: Warner Business Books, 2005), p. 42.

5. Trump, *Trump: The Art of the Deal*, p. 48.

6. Robert Slater, *No Such Thing as Over-Exposure: Inside the Life and Celebrity of Donald Trump* (Upper Saddle, N. J.: Pearson Education, Inc., 2005), p. 47.

7. Blair, pp. 6–7.

8. Slater, p. 44.

9. Harry Hurt III, *Lost Tycoon: the Many Lives of Donald J. Trump* (New York: W. W. Norton & Co., 1993), p. 76.

10. Blair, p. 19.

11. Donald J. Trump, with Meredith McIver, *Trump: Think Like a Billionaire* (New York: Random House, 2004), p. xiv.

12. Hurt III, p. 77.

13. Blair, p. 9.

14. Hurt III, p. 76.

15. O'Brien, p. 49.

16. Trump, *Trump: The Art of the Deal*, p. 50.

17. Slater, p. 43.

18. Blair, p. 12.

19. Hurt III, p. 77.

20. Trump, *Trump: The Art of the Deal*, p. 50.

Chapter 3. An Able Apprentice

1. Jerome Tuccille, *Trump* (New York: Jove Books, 1988), p. 27.

2. E. D. Hill, *Going Places: How America's Best and*

Brightest Got Started Down the Road of Life (New York: Regan Books, 2005), p. 289.

3. Donald J. Trump, with Tony Schwartz, *Trump: The Art of the Deal* (New York: Random House, 1987), p. 53.

4. Wayne Barrett, *Trump: The Deals and the Downfall* (New York: HarperCollins, 1992), p. 78.

5. Harry Hurt III, *Lost Tycoon: The Many Lives of Donald J. Trump* (New York: W. W. Norton & Co., 1993), p. 76.

6. Hill, p. 290.

7. Timothy L. O'Brien, *TrumpNation: The Art of Being The Donald* (New York: Warner Business Books, 2005), p. 49.

8. Gwenda Blair, *The Trumps: Three Generations That Built an Empire* (New York: Simon & Schuster, 2000), p. 245.

9. Barrett, p. 75.

10. Blair, p. 248.

11. Ibid., pp. 248–249.

12. Trump, p. 45.

13. Gwenda Blair, *Donald Trump: Master Apprentice* (New York: Simon & Schuster, 2005), p. 23.

14. Trump, p. 64.

15. Ibid., pp. 64–65.

16. Hurt III, p. 81.

17. O'Brien, p. 52.

18. Blair, *Donald Trump: Master Apprentice*, p. 24.

19. Ibid., p. 22.

20. Hill, p. 290.

21. Blair, *The Trumps: Three Generations That Built an Empire*, p. 249.

22. Trump, p. 45.

23. Blair, *The Trumps: Three Generations That Built an Empire*, p. 251.

24. Blair, Donald *Trump: Master Apprentice*, p. 23.

Chapter 4. The Big Time

1. Donald J. Trump, with Tony Schwartz, *Trump: The Art of the Deal* (New York: Random House, 1987), p. 70.

2. Gwenda Blair, *The Trumps: Three Generations That Built an Empire* (New York: Simon & Schuster, 2000), p. 255.

3. Ibid., p. 260.

4. Gwenda Blair, Donald *Trump: Master Apprentice* (New York: Simon & Schuster, 2005), p. 42.

5. Robert Slater, *No Such Thing as Over-Exposure: Inside the Life and Celebrity of Donald Trump* (Upper Saddle, N. J.: Pearson Education, Inc., 2005), p. 11.

6. Ibid., p. 60.

7. Ibid., p. 61.

8. Trump, *Trump: The Art of the Deal*, p. 82.

9. Donald J. Trump, with Meredith McIver, *Trump: How to Get Rich* (New York: Random House, 2004), p. 13.

10. Slater, p. 59.

11. Trump, *Trump: The Art of the Deal*, p. 85.

12. Slater, pp. 61–62.

13. Harry Hurt III, *Lost Tycoon: The Many Lives of Donald J. Trump* (New York: W.W. Norton & Co., 1993), pp. 88–89.

14. Trump, *Trump: The Art of the Deal,* p. 91.

15. Hurt III, p. 83.

16. Blair, *Donald Trump: Master Apprentice,* p. 54.

17. Norman King, *Ivana Trump: A Very Unauthorized Biography* (New York: Carroll & Graf Publishers, Inc., 1990), p 72.

18. Hurt III, p. 102.

19. King, p. 67.

20. Blair, *Donald Trump: Master Apprentice,* p. 67.

21. King, p. 68.

22. Blair, *Donald Trump: Master Apprentice,* p. 64.

23. Ibid.

24. Trump, *Trump: How to Get Rich,* p. 206.

25. Blair, *Donald Trump: Master Apprentice,* p. 69.

26. Ibid.

27. Hurt III, p. 114.

28. Blair, *Donald Trump: Master Apprentice,* p. 69.

29. Jerome Tuccille, *Trump* (New York: Jove Books, 1988), pp. 169–170.

30. Slater, p. 62.

Chapter 5. Tower of Treats

1. Donald J. Trump, with Kate Bohner, *Trump: The Art of the Comeback* (New York: Random House, 1997), p. 109.

2. Norman King, *Ivana Trump: A Very Unauthorized Biography* (New York: Carroll & Graf Publishers, Inc., 1990), p. 96.

3. Donald J. Trump, with Tony Schwartz, *Trump: The Art of the Deal* (New York: Random House, 1987), p. 32.

4. Ibid., p. 99.

5. Harry Hurt III, *Lost Tycoon: The Many Lives of Donald J. Trump* (New York: W. W. Norton & Co., 1993), p. 115.

6. William E. Geist, "The Expanding Empire of Donald Trump," *The New York Times Magazine*, April 8, 1984, section 6, page 28, column 2.

7. Trump, *Trump: The Art of the Deal*, p. 101.

8. Ibid., p. 110.

9. Ibid., p. 111.

10. Sy Rubin, photographs, and Jonathan Mandell, text, *Trump Tower* (Secaucus, N. J.: Lyle Stuart Inc., 1984), p. 29.

11. Hurt III, p. 117.

12. Rubin and Mandell, p. 36.

13. Ada Louise Huxtable, "A New York Blockbuster of Superior Design," *The New York Times*, July 1, 1979, p. D25.

14. Trump, *Trump: The Art of the Deal*, p. 116.

15. Ibid., p. 117.

16. Ibid., p. 8.

17. King, p. 100.

18. Hurt III, p. 128.

19. Trump, *Trump: The Art of the Deal*, p. 39.

20. Ibid., p. 40.

21. Geist, p. 28.

22. Timothy L. O'Brien, *TrumpNation: The Art of Being The Donald* (New York: Warner Business Books, 2005), p. 66.

23. Gwenda Blair, *Donald Trump: Master Apprentice* (New York: Simon & Schuster, 2005), p. 60.

24. Ibid.

25. Trump, *Trump: The Art of the Deal*, p. 121.

26. King, pp. 105–106.

27. Geist, p. 28.

28. Trump, *Trump: The Art of the Deal*, p. 30.

Chapter 6. The Fast Lane

1. Harry Hurt III, *Lost Tycoon: The Many Lives of Donald J. Trump* (New York: W. W. Norton & Co., 1993), p. 144.

2. Timothy L. O'Brien, *TrumpNation: The Art of Being The Donald* (New York: Warner Business Books, 2005), p. 89.

3. Gwenda Blair, *Donald Trump: Master Apprentice* (New York: Simon & Schuster, 2005), p. 101.

4. O'Brien, p. 90.

5. William E. Geist, "The Expanding Empire of Donald Trump," *The New York Times Magazine*, April 8, 1984, p. 28, <http://select.nytimes.com> (September 14, 2007).

6. Donald J. Trump, with Charles Leerhsen, *Trump: Surviving at the Top* (New York: Random House, 1990), p. 10.

7. Donald J. Trump, with Tony Schwartz, *Trump: The Art of the Deal* (New York: Random House, 1987), p. 9.

8. Wayne Barrett, *Trump: The Deals and the Downfall* (New York: HarperCollins, 1992), p. 5.

9. Trump, *The Art of the Deal*, p. 177.

10. Ibid., pp. 388–389.

11. Robert Slater, *No Such Thing as Over-Exposure: Inside the Life and Celebrity of Donald Trump* (Upper Saddle, N. J.: Pearson Education, Inc., 2005), p. 69.

12. Geist.

13. Hurt III, p. 176.

14. Trump, *Surviving at the Top*, p. 55.

15. Slater, p. 105.

16. O'Brien, p. 97.

17. John R. O'Donnell, with James Rutherford, *Trumped! The Inside Story of the Real Donald Trump—His Cunning Rise and Spectacular Fall* (New York: Simon & Schuster, 1991), p. 133.

18. Trump, *Surviving at the Top*, p. 155.

19. Blair, p. 147.

20. William H. Meyers, "Stalking the Plaza," *The New York Times*, September 25, 1988, p. 1, <http://select.nytimes.com/search> (October 23, 2007).

21. Trump, *Surviving at the Top*, p. 19.

22. Lenny Glynn, "Trump's Taj—Open at Last, With a Scary Appetite," *The New York Times*, April 8, 1990, <http://select.nytimes.com> (September 15, 2007).

Chapter 7. A House of Cards

1. Donald J. Trump, with Charles Leerhsen, *Trump: Surviving at the Top* (New York: Random House, 1990), pp. 166–167.

2. Robert Slater, *No Such Thing as Over-Exposure: Inside the Life and Celebrity of Donald Trump* (Upper Saddle, N. J.: Pearson Education, Inc., 2005), p. 102.

3. Diana B. Henriques, "Bank Talks Confirmed by

Trump," *The New York Times*, June 5, 1990, p. 1, <http://select.nytimes.com> (October 23, 2007).

4. Slater, p. 112.

5. John R. O'Donnell, with James Rutherford, *Trumped! The Inside Story of the Real Donald Trump—His Cunning Rise and Spectacular Fall* (New York: Simon & Schuster, 1991), p. 332.

6. Donald J. Trump, with Kate Bohner, *Trump: The Art of the Comeback* (New York: Random House, 1997), p. 4.

7. Slater, p. 103.

8. Trump, *Trump: Surviving at the Top*, p. 60.

9. Trump, *Trump: The Art of the Comeback*, p. 3.

10. Gwenda Blair, *Donald Trump: Master Apprentice* (New York: Simon & Schuster, 2005), p. 172.

11. Trump, *Trump: The Art of the Comeback*, p. 16.

12. Ibid., p. 17.

13. Timothy L. O'Brien, *TrumpNation: The Art of Being The Donald* (New York: Warner Business Books, 2005), p. 137.

14. Trump, *Trump: The Art of the Comeback*, pp. 14–15.

15. Blair, p. 175.

16. Trump, *Trump: Surviving at the Top*, p. 5.

17. Ibid.

18. O'Brien, pp. 139, 143.

19. Ibid., p. 157.

20. Trump, *Trump: Surviving at the Top*, p. 48.

21. Ibid., pp. 82–83.

22. Blair, p. 197.

23. Donald J. Trump, with Meredith McIver, *Trump: How to Get Rich* (New York: Random House, 2004), p. 43.

24. Slater, p. 116.

25. Trump, *Trump: The Art of the Comeback*, p. xix.

Chapter 8. Comeback

1. Donald J. Trump, with Meredith McIver, *Trump: Think Like a Billionaire* (New York: Random House, 2004), p. xiv.

2. Donald J. Trump, with Kate Bohner, *Trump: The Art of the Comeback* (New York: Random House, 1997), p. 8.

3. Donald J. Trump, with Charles Leerhsen, *Trump: Surviving at the Top* (New York: Random House, 1990), p.120.

4. Ibid., pp. 12–13.

5. John R. O'Donnell, with James Rutherford, *Trumped! The Inside Story of the Real Donald Trump—His Cunning Rise and Spectacular Fall* (New York: Simon & Schuster, 1991), p. 226.

6. Trump, *Trump: The Art of the Comeback*, pp. 46–47.

7. Donald J. Trump, with Meredith McIver, *Trump: How to Get Rich* (New York: Random House, 2004), p. 121.

8. Ibid., p. 119.

9. Ibid., p. 121.

10. Ibid., p. 51.

11. Trump, *Trump: Think Like a Billionaire*, p. 63.

12. Ibid., p. 168.

13. Trump, *Trump: The Art of the Comeback*, p. 140.

14. Trump, *Trump: How to Get Rich*, p. 160.

15. Ibid.

16. Trump, *Trump: Surviving at the Top*, p. 218.

17. Amazon.com, *The America We Deserve*, book description.

18. Trump, *How to Get Rich*, p. 57.

19. Charles V. Bagli, "Trump Starts a New Tower Near the U.N.," *The New York Times*, October 16, 1998, <http://select.nytimes.com> (October 23, 2007).

20. Trump, *Trump: Surviving at the Top*, p. 88.

21. Ibid., p. 64.

22. Timothy L. O'Brien, *TrumpNation: The Art of Being The Donald* (New York: Warner Business Books, 2005), p. 172.

23. Trump, Trump: *How to Get Rich*, pp. 238–239.

24. William E. Geist, "The Expanding Empire of Donald Trump," *The New York Times Magazine*, April 8, 1984, p. 28, <http://select.nytimes.com> (September 14, 2007).

25. Ibid., and Slater, p. 25.

Chapter 9. A New Career

1. Donald J. Trump, with Meredith McIver, *Trump: How to Get Rich* (New York: Random House, 2004), p. 214.

2. Timothy L. O'Brien, *TrumpNation: The Art of Being The Donald* (New York: Warner Business Books, 2005), p. 15.

3. Ibid., p. 16.

4. Bill Rancic, *You're Hired: How to Succeed in Business and Life* (New York: Harper Business, 2004), p. 143.

5. Ibid., p. 148.

6. Ibid., p. 1.

7. Trump, p. 215.

8. Ibid., p. 220.

9. Ibid., p. 225.

10. Timothy L. O'Brien and Eric Dash, "The Midas Touch, With Spin on It," *The New York Times*, September 8, 2004, <http://select.nytimes.com> (October 23, 2007).

11. "Mark Burnett on *The Apprentice*," Disc 5: Bonus Features, *The Apprentice, The Complete First Season,* DVD (Universal City, Calif.: Universal Studios, 2004).

12. O'Brien, *TrumpNation: The Art of Being The Donald,* p. 33.

13. Ibid., p. 26.

14. "The Boss: Donald Trump on The Apprentice," Disc 5: Bonus Features, *The Apprentice, The Complete First Season,* DVD (Universal City, Calif.: Universal Studios, 2004).

15. Amazon.com, Trump: *How to Get Rich, Publisher's Weekly* review.

16. E. D. Hill, *Going Places: How America's Best and Brightest Got Started Down the Road of Life* (New York: Regan Books, 2005), p. 289.

Chapter 10. New Horizons

1. Joyce Waller, "Melania Knauss and Donald Trump Wed," *The New York Times*, January 23, 2005, <http://www.nytimes.com/2005/01/23/nyregion/23xtrump.html> (October 23, 2007).

2. Amazon.com, *Why We Want You to be Rich: Two Men—One Message, Publisher's Weekly* review.

3. Mathew Boyle, "The Donald," *Fortune*, Vol. 155, No. 5, March 19, 2007, p. 70.

4. Donald J. Trump, with Meredith McIver, *Trump: How to Get Rich* (New York: Random House, 2004), p. 151.

5. Ibid.

6. Ibid.

7. Gwenda Blair, *Donald Trump: Master Apprentice* (New York: Simon & Schuster, 2005), p. 116.

8. Donald J. Trump, with Charles Leerhsen, *Trump: Surviving at the Top* (New York: Random House, 1990), p. 84.

9. Timothy L. O'Brien, *TrumpNation: The Art of Being The Donald* (New York: Warner Business Books, 2005), p. 195.

10. Trump, *Trump: Surviving at the Top*, pp. 213–215.

11. Ibid., p. 228.

12. Blair, pp. 114–115.

13. Ibid., p. 117.

14. Rick Marin, "Hug-Hug, Kiss-Kiss: It's a Jungle Out There," *The New York Times*, September 19, 1999, <http://select.nytimes.com> (October 23, 2007).

15. Donald J. Trump, with Kate Bohner, *Trump: The Art of the Comeback* (New York: Random House, 1997), p. 176.

16. Stephanie Fitch, "How Much is He Worth?" *Forbes*, October 9, 2006, p. 1, <http://www.forbes.com> (October 23, 2007).

17. O'Brien, p. 156

18. Donald J. Trump, with Tony Schwartz, *Trump: The Art of the Deal* (New York: Random House, 1987), p. 242.

19. Donald J. Trump, with Meredith McIver, *Trump: Think Like a Billionaire* (New York: Random House, 2004), p. 135.

FURTHER READING

Blair, Gwenda. *Donald Trump: Master Apprentice.* New York: Simon & Schuster, 2005.

Blair, Gwenda. *The Trumps: Three Generations That Built an Empire.* New York: Simon & Schuster, 2001.

Payment, Simone. *Donald Trump: Profile of a Real Estate Tycoon.* New York: Rosen Publishing Group, 2007.

Rancic, Bill, with Karen Soenen. *Beyond the Lemonade Stand: Starting Small to Make It Big!* New York: Razorbill/Penguin Group, 2005.

Trump, Donald J., with Meredith McIver. *Trump: Think Like a Billionaire.* New York: Random House, 2004.

Trump, Donald J., with Tony Schwartz. *Trump: The Art of the Deal.* New York: Random House, 2005.

INTERNET ADDRESSES

Donald Trump official Web site
http://www.trump.com

The Apprentice NBC Web site
http://www.nbc.com/The_Apprentice/

Trump University
http://www.trumpuniversity.com/

INDEX